AN ORTHODOX
PRAYER BOOK

Title: An Orthodox Prayer Book

Edition: Second, November 2013

Translation: The text of *An Orthodox Prayer Book* is based on the order of *The Prayer Book*, Nea Moni, Mount Athos, with emendations and additions, as well as that of the V. Rev. Archimandrite Ephrem Lash with modifications by Rev. Fr. Michael Monos. The translation of Holy Scripture used herein is from the Eastern Orthodox Bible, http://www.orthodoxanswers.org/eob/. *Occasional Prayers* come from a variety of uncredited sources in the public domain.

ISBN: 978-1-939028105 (Hardcover Edition)

Publisher: Newrome Press LLC, PO Box 30608, Columbia, MO 65205

Design: The Rev. Fr. Michael Monos. All icons (*except line art icons*) are by Michael Hadjimichael, and used herein by permission. http://www.michaelhadjimichael.com

Website: http://www.newromepress.com

AN ORTHODOX
PRAYER BOOK

NEWROME
PRESS

*S*ince God is continuously present, why do you worry? For in Him we live and move. We are carried in His arms. We breathe God; we are vested with God; we touch God; we consume God in Mystery. Wherever you turn, wherever you look, God is everywhere: in the heavens, on the earth, in the abysses, in the trees, within the rocks, in your nous, in your heart. So can't He see that you are suffering, that you are going through tribulations? Tell Him your grievances and you will see consolation, you will see healing which will heal not only the body, but even more so the passions of your soul.

The Letters of Elder Joseph the Hesychast
Thirtieth Letter

Christ, the Almighty

CONTENTS

AN ORTHODOX PRAYER BOOK

Knowledge of God is vision of God, because spiritual knowledge, not natural knowledge, knows God. For natural knowledge is discernment which can tell good from bad, and all people have it, but spiritual knowledge comes from spiritual work, and coming to "know thyself." All these things happen to us by the grace of God through prayer. The grace of God is beheld noetically and is known by the perception of the nous during prayer. There are many ways to pray. All of them are good – if one does not know any better and prays with simplicity...

The Letters of Elder Joseph the Hesychast
Sixty-third Letter

INTRODUCTION

THE ATTENDANTS OF PRIESTMONK SPYRIDON

NEW SKETE, HOLY MOUNT ATHOS, GREECE

In Memory of Blessed Spiritual Fathers who guide us on the true paths of Righteousness by the spiritual grace Of God.:

Prayer, according to St. John Chrysostomos, is a large and mighty weapon, a great possession, an insurance of the meeting of man with God; it is a medicine, a never ending richness; it is the veins of the soul through which the grace of God flows freely, an invitation to eternal life. Prayer makes man like the Angels. It is man's conversation with God.

"Nothing has it's measure. Nothing can compare with it," writes the holy Father.

Prayer is a skill, and thus it requires practice and continued effort. It must be offered with a zealous soul and with deep concentration so that we realize what exactly we are doing, before whom we stand and with whom we are conversing.

"Pray without ceasing" St. Paul tells us. (1 Thess. 5: 5-17) In joy, in sorrow, with patience, endurance, with contrition and humility.

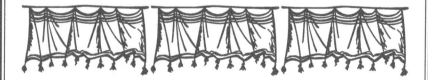

MORNING PRAYERS

After rising from sleep, stand with reverence and fear of God, make the sign of the cross, and say:

In the name of the Father, and the Son, and the Holy Spirit. Amen.

Glory to you, our God, glory to you.

Heavenly King, comforter, the Spirit of truth, who are present everywhere filling all things, Treasury of good things and Giver of life, come and dwell in us, Cleanse us of every stain, and save our souls, gracious Lord.

Holy God, Holy Mighty, Holy Immortal, have mercy on us. (*x3*)

Glory to the Father, and the Son, and the Holy Spirit, now and forever and to the ages of ages. Amen.

All-holy Trinity, have mercy on us. Lord, forgive our sins. Master, pardon our transgressions. Holy One, visit and heal our infirmities for the glory of Your name.

Lord, have mercy. *(x3)* Glory to the Father, and the Son, and the Holy Spirit, now and forever and to the ages of ages. Amen.

Our Father, who art in heaven, hallowed be Thy name. Thy kingdom come. Thy will be done, on earth as it is in heaven. Give us this day our daily bread; and forgive us our trespasses, as we forgive those who trespass against us. And lead us not into temptation, but deliver us from the evil one.

Through the prayers of our Holy Fathers, Lord Jesus Christ our God, have mercy upon us and save us. Amen.

Having risen from sleep, we fall down before you. O good One, and sing to you, mighty One, the angelic hymn: Holy, holy, holy are you, O God. Through the prayers of the Theotokos, have mercy on us.

Glory to the Father and the Son and the Holy Spirit.

Having aroused me from sleep and bed, O Lord, enlighten my mind and open my heart and lips that I may sing to you, Holy, holy, holy, are you, O God. Through the prayers of the Theotokos, have mercy on us. Now and forever and to the ages of ages. Amen.

Suddenly the judge will come and everyone's deeds will be revealed. But with fear we cry out in the middle of the night: Holy, holy, holy are you, O God, through the prayers of the Theotokos, have mercy on us.

Lord, have mercy. *(x12)*

Thanksgiving Prayer

As I rise from sleep, I thank you, Holy Trinity, for because of your great goodness and patience, you were not angry with me, an idler and sinner, nor have you destroyed me in my sins, but have shown your usual love for me. When I was prostrate in despair, you raised me up to glorify your power. Now enlighten my mind's eye, open my mouth to study your words and understand your commandments, to do your will and sing to you in heartfelt adoration, and praise your most holy name, of the Father and the Son and the Holy Spirit, now and forever and to the ages of ages. Amen.

Another Prayer

Glory to you, King, God almighty, who through your divine and loving providence have consented that I, an unworthy sinner, should rise from sleep and obtain entrance into your holy house. Accept, Lord, the voice of my prayer as you accept those of your holy and spiritual powers – not from defiled lips, but from a pure heart and a humble spirit. May I offer you praise, so that with the bright lamp of my soul, I may become a companion of the wise virgins and glorify you, God the Word, who is glorified in the Father and the Spirit. Amen.

Come, let us worship and fall down before the King, our God.

Come, let us worship and fall down before Christ, the King, our God.

Come, let us worship and fall down before Christ himself, the King, our God.

Psalm 50

Have mercy upon me, O God, according to your great mercy; according to the multitude of your compassions blot out my transgression.

Wash me thoroughly from my iniquity and cleanse me from my sin.

For I am conscious of my iniquity; and my sin is continually before me.

Against you alone have I sinned and done evil before you: that you might be justified in your sayings and overcome in your judgments.

For, behold, I was conceived in iniquities and in sins did my mother conceive me.

For, behold, you love truth: you have manifested to me the secret and hidden things of your wisdom.

You shall sprinkle me with hyssop and I shall be purified: you shall wash me and I shall be made whiter than snow.

You shall cause me to hear gladness and joy: the afflicted bones shall rejoice.

Turn away your face from my sins and blot out all my iniquities.

Create in me a clean heart, O God; and renew a right spirit in my inner being.

Do not cast me away from your presence; and do not remove your holy Spirit from me.

Restore to me the joy of your salvation: establish me with your guiding Spirit.

Then will I teach transgressors your ways; and ungodly men shall return to you.

Deliver me from blood guiltiness, O God, the God of my salvation: then my tongue shall joyfully declare your righteousness.

O Lord, you shall open my lips; and my mouth shall declare your praise.

If you desired sacrifice, I would have given it: you will not take pleasure in whole-burnt-offerings.

Sacrifice to God is a broken spirit: a broken and humbled heart God will not despise.

Do good, O Lord, to Zion in your good pleasure; Let the walls of Jerusalem be rebuilt.

Then shall you be pleased with a sacrifice of righteousness, with offering and whole-burnt sacrifices: then shall they offer calves upon your altar.

THE SYMBOL OF FAITH

I believe in one God, Father Almighty, Creator of heaven and earth and of all things visible and invisible.

And in one Lord Jesus Christ, the only-begotten Son of God, begotten of the Father before all ages. Light of Light, true God of true God, begotten not created, of one essence with the Father through Whom all things were made.

Who for us men and for our salvation came down from heaven and was incarnate of the Holy Spirit and the Virgin Mary and became man.

He was crucified for us under Pontius Pilate. He suffered and was buried.

And He rose on the third day, according to the Scriptures.

He ascended into heaven and is seated at the right hand of the Father.

And He will come again with glory to judge the living and dead. His kingdom shall have no end.

And in the Holy Spirit, the Lord, the Creator of life, Who proceeds from the Father, Who together with the Father and the Son is worshiped and glorified, Who spoke through the prophets.

In one, holy, catholic, and apostolic Church.

I confess one baptism for the forgiveness of sins.

I look for the resurrection of the dead and the life of the age to come. Amen.

Glory to the Father and to the Son and to the Holy Spirit. Now and forever and to the ages of ages. Amen. Lord, have mercy. (x3)

Through the prayers of our Holy Fathers, Lord Jesus Christ our God, have mercy upon us and save us. Amen.

ATTENTION, many Christians have the blessed habit of reading the SIX PSALMS and the small DOXOLOGY, in their morning praise to God.

THE SIX PSALMS

Holy God, Holy Mighty, Holy Immortal, have mercy on us *(x3)*.

*Glory to the Father and the Son and the Holy Spirit,
now and forever and to the ages of ages. Amen.*

All-holy Trinity, have mercy on us. Lord, forgive our sins. Master, pardon our transgressions. Holy One, visit and heal our infirmities for the glory of Your name.

Lord, have mercy. *(x3)*

*Glory to the Father and the Son and the Holy Spirit,
now and forever and to the ages of ages. Amen.*

Our Father, who art in heaven, hallowed be Thy name. Thy kingdom come. Thy will be done, on earth as it is in heaven. Give us this day our daily bread; and forgive us our trespasses, as we forgive those who trespass against us. And lead us not into temptation, but deliver us from the evil one.

Through the prayers of the holy fathers, Lord Jesus Christ our God, have mercy upon us and save us. Amen.

Lord save your people and bless your inheritance. Grant victory to the Orthodox over their adversaries and guard your commonwealth with your cross.

Glory to the Father and the Son and the Holy Spirit.

You were lifted up upon the cross of your own will, Christ our God. Grant your mercy upon the new commonwealth that bears your name. In strength make glad the orthodox, giving them victory over their adversaries. May they have your alliance as a weapon of peace, and an invincible trophy. Now and forever and to the ages of ages. Amen.

O awesome and ever-present protection,
do not overlook, O gracious one, our supplications.

Most praised Theotokos, establish the Orthodox people, save those whom you have called to govern and grant them victory from above, for you have given birth to God, only blessed one.

Lord, have mercy. *(x3)*

Glory to God in the highest, and on earth peace, good will among all people. *(x3)*

Lord open my lips and my mouth shall proclaim your praise. *(x2)*

Psalm 3

O Lord, why are those who afflict me multiplied? Many rise up against me.

Many say concerning my soul, There is no deliverance for him in his God.

But you, O Lord, are my helper: my glory and the one that lifts up my head.

I cried to the Lord with my voice, He heard me out of his holy mountain.

I lay down and slept; I awoke; for the Lord will help me.

I will not be afraid of ten thousands of people, who beset me round about.

Arise, Lord; deliver me, my God: for you have stricken all who were without cause my enemies; you have broken the teeth of sinners.

Deliverance is the Lord's and your blessing is upon your people.

And again

I lay down and slept; I awoke; for the Lord will help me. (*x2*)

Psalm 37

O Lord, rebuke me not in your wrath, neither chasten me in your anger.

For your weapons are fixed in me, and you have pressed your hand heavily upon me.

For there is no health in my flesh because of your anger; there is no peace to my bones because of my sins.

For my transgressions have gone over my head: they have pressed heavily upon me like a weighty burden.

My bruises have become foul and corrupt, because of my foolishness.

I have been wretched and bowed down continually: I went with a mourning countenance all the day.

For my soul is filled with delusions; and there is no health in my flesh.

I have been afflicted and extremely downcast: I have groaned for the turmoil of my heart.

But all my desire is before you; and my groaning is not hidden from you.

My heart is troubled, my strength has failed me; and the light of my eyes is not with me.

My friends and my neighbors drew near before me and stood still; and my nearest of kin stood afar off.

While those who pressed hard upon me sought my soul: and those who sought to hurt me spoke vanities, they devised deceits all the day.

But I, as a deaf man, heard not; and I was as a speechless man not opening his mouth.

I was as a man that hears not, and who has no reproofs in his mouth.

For I hoped in you, O Lord: you will hear, O Lord my God.

For I said: for fear that my enemies rejoice against me: for when my feet were moved, they spoke with pride against me.

For I am ready for plagues, and my grief is continually before me.

For I will declare my iniquity, and be distressed for my sin.

But my enemies live and they are mightier than I: those who hate me unjustly have multiplied.

Those who reward evil for good slandered me; because I followed righteousness; they cast me forth, the beloved, as a loathsome carcass.

Forsake me not, O Lord my God: depart not from me.

Draw near to my help, O Lord of my salvation.

And again

Forsake me not, O Lord my God: depart not from me.

Draw near to my help, O Lord of my salvation.

Psalm 62

O God, my God, I cry to you in the early morning; my soul has thirsted for you: how often has my flesh longed after you, in a barren, parched and dry land!

Thus have I appeared before you in the sanctuary, that I might see your power and your glory.

For your mercy is better than life: my lips shall praise you.

Thus will I bless you during my life: I will lift up my hands in your name.

Let my soul be filled as with marrow and fatness; and my joyful lips shall praise your name.

For as much as I have remembered you on my bed: in the early seasons I have meditated on you.

For you have been my helper and in the shelter of your wings will I rejoice.

My soul has kept very close to you: your right hand has upheld me.

But they vainly sought after my soul; they shall go into the lowest parts of the earth.

They shall be delivered up to the power of the sword; they shall be portions for foxes.

But the king shall rejoice in God; every one that swears by him shall be praised; for the mouth of those who speak unjust things has been stopped.

And again

In the early seasons I have meditated on you.

For you have been my helper and in the shelter of your wings will I rejoice.

My soul has kept very close to you: your right hand has upheld me.

Alleluia, alleluia, alleluia, glory to You, O God.

Lord have mercy. *(x3)*

Glory to the Father, and the Son, and the Holy Spirit, both now and ever and to the ages of ages. Amen.

Psalm 87

O Lord God of my salvation, I have cried by day and in the night before you.

Let my prayer come in before you; incline your ear to my supplication, O Lord.

For my soul is filled with troubles and my life has drawn near to hades.

I have been counted with those who go down to the pit; I became as a man without help;

Free among the dead, as the slain ones cast out, who sleep in the tomb; whom you remember no more; and they are rejected from your hand.

They laid me in the lowest pit, in dark places and in the shadow of death.

Your wrath has pressed heavily upon me and you have engulfed me with all your smoke.

You have removed my acquaintances far from me; they have made me an abomination to themselves; I have been delivered up and have not gone forth.

My eyes are dimmed from poverty; but I cried to you, O Lord, all the day; I spread forth my hands to you.

Will you work wonders for the dead? Or shall physicians raise them up, so that they may praise you?

Shall any one declare your mercy in the tomb? And your truth in destruction?

Shall your wonders be known in darkness? And your righteousness in a forgotten land?

But I cried to you, O Lord; and in the morning shall my prayer be presented to you.

Why then, O Lord, do you reject my prayer and turn your face away from me?

I am poor and in troubles from my youth; and having been exalted, I was brought low and into despair.

Your wrath has passed over me; and your terrors have greatly distressed me.

They surrounded me like water; all the day they beset me together.

You have put far from me every friend and my acquaintances because of my wretchedness.

And again

O Lord God of my salvation, I have cried by day and in the night before you.

Let my prayer come in before you; incline your ear to my supplication, O Lord.

Psalm 102

Bless the Lord, O my soul; and all that is within me, bless his holy name.

Bless the Lord, O my soul and forget not all his praises:

Who forgives all your transgressions, who heals all your diseases;

Who redeems your life from corruption; who crowns you with mercy and compassion;

Who satisfies your desire with good things: so that your youth shall be renewed like that of the eagle.

The Lord executes mercy and judgment for all that are injured.

He made known his ways to Moses, his will to the children of Israel.

The Lord is compassionate and merciful, long-suffering and full of mercy.

He will not be always angry; neither will he be wrathful for ever.

He has not dealt with us according to our sins, nor repaid us according to our iniquities.

For as the heaven is high above the earth, so has the Lord increased his mercy toward those who fear him.

As far as the east is from the west, so far has he removed our transgressions from us.

As a father pities his children, the Lord pities those who fear him.

For he knows our frame: remember that we are dust.

As for man, his days are as grass; as a flower of the field, so shall he flourish.

For the wind passes over it and it shall not be; it shall know its place no more.

But the mercy of the Lord is from generation to generation upon those who fear him, and his righteousness to children's children;

To those who keep his covenant and remember his commandments to do them.

The Lord has prepared his throne in the heaven; and his kingdom rules over all.

Bless the Lord, all you his angels, mighty in strength, who perform his bidding, ready to hearken to the voice of his words.

Bless the Lord, all you his hosts; his ministers that do his will.

Bless the Lord, all his works, in every place of his dominion: bless the Lord, O my soul!

And again

In every place of his dominion: bless the Lord, O my soul!

Psalm 142

O Lord, attend to my prayer: hearken to my supplication in your truth; hear me in your righteousness.

Do not enter into judgment with your servant, for in your sight shall no man living be justified.

For the enemy has persecuted my soul; he has brought my life down to the ground; he has made me to dwell in a dark place, as those who have been long dead.

Therefore my spirit was grieved in me; my heart was troubled within me.

I remembered the days of old; and I meditated on all your doings: yes, I meditated on the works of your hands.

I spread forth my hands to you; my soul thirsts for you, as a dry land.

Hear me speedily, O Lord; my spirit has failed; turn not away your face from me, else I shall be like to those who go down to the pit.

Cause me to hear your mercy in the morning; for I have hoped in you; make known to me, O Lord, the way by which I should walk; for I have lifted up my soul to you.

Deliver me from my enemies, O Lord; for I have fled to you for refuge.

Teach me to do your will; for you are my God; your good Spirit shall guide me in the straight way.

You shall revive me, O Lord, for your name's sake; in your righteousness you shall bring my soul out of affliction.

In your mercy you will destroy my enemies and destroy all those who afflict my soul, for I am your servant.

And again

Hear me in your righteousness. Do not enter into judgment with your servant. *(x2)*

Your good Spirit shall guide me in the straight way.

Glory to the Father, and the Son, and the Holy Spirit, both now and ever and to the ages of ages. Amen.

Alleluia, alleluia, alleluia, glory to You, O God. *(x3)* Our hope, O Lord, glory to You.

DOXOLOGY
Small

Glory to God in the highest, and on earth peace, goodwill among men.

We praise you, we bless you, we worship you, we glorify you, we give you thanks for your great glory.

Lord, King, God of heaven, Father almighty: Lord, only-begotten Son, Jesus Christ and Holy Spirit.

Lord God, Lamb of God, Son of the Father, who take away the sin of the world, have mercy on us; you take away the sins of the world.

Receive our prayer, you who sit on the right hand of the Father, and have mercy on us.

For you alone are holy, you alone are Lord, Jesus Christ, to the glory of God the Father. Amen.

Every day I will bless you, and praise your name for ever and to the ages of ages.

Lord, you have been our refuge from generation to generation. I said, Lord, have mercy on me, heal my soul, for I have sinned against you.

Lord, I have run to you for refuge: teach me to do your will, for you are my God.

For with you is the source of life: and in your light we shall see light. Continue your mercy towards those who know you. Grant, Lord, this day to keep us without sin.

Blessed are you, O Lord, the God of our fathers, and praised and glorified your name to the ages. Amen.

May your mercy, O Lord, be upon us, as we have put our hope in you.

Blessed are you, Lord, teach me your statutes. Blessed are you, Master, make me understand your statutes. Blessed are you, Holy One, enlighten me with your statutes.

Lord, your mercy is for ever; do not scorn the work of your hands.

To you praise is due, to you song is due, to you glory is due, Father, Son and Holy Spirit, now and for ever, and to the ages of ages. Amen.

Glory to the Father and to the Son and to the Holy Spirit, now and forever, and unto the ages of ages. Amen. Lord have mercy. *(x3)*

Through the prayers of the holy fathers, Lord Jesus Christ our God, have mercy on us and save us. Amen.

κατευ-
θυνθήτω   ὡς θυμίαμα
ἡ προ-   ἐνώπιόν
σευχή μου   σου

SERVICE of VESPERS

Evening Service

In the name of the Father, and the Son, and the Holy Spirit. Amen.

Come, let us worship and fall down before the King, our God.

Come, let us worship and fall down before Christ the King, our God.

Come, let us worship and fall down before Christ himself, the King and our God.

Psalm 103

Bless the Lord, O my soul. O Lord my God, you are very great; you have clothed yourself with praise and honor:

You robe yourself with light as with a garment; spreading out the heaven as a curtain.

Who covers his chambers with waters; who makes the clouds his chariot; who walks on the wings of the wind.

Who makes his angels spirits and his ministers a flaming fire.

Who establishes the earth on her sure foundation: it shall not be moved for ever.

The deep, as it were a garment, is his covering: the waters stood above the hills.

At your rebuke they shall flee; at the voice of your thunder they shall be alarmed.

They go up to the mountains and down to the plains, to the place which you have founded for them.

You have set a bound which they shall not pass, neither shall they return to cover the earth.

He sends forth his fountains among the valleys: the waters shall run between the mountains.

They shall give drink to all the wild beasts of the field: the wild donkeys shall take of them to quench their thirst.

By them shall the birds of the sky dwell: they shall utter a voice out of the midst of the rocks.

He waters the mountains from his chambers: the earth shall be satisfied with the fruit of your works.

He makes grass to grow for the cattle and plants for the service of men, to bring bread out of the earth;

And wine makes glad the heart of man, to make his face cheerful with oil: bread strengthens man's heart.

The trees of the plain shall be full of sap; even the cedars of Lebanon which he planted.

There the sparrows will build their nests; the stork takes the lead among them.

The high mountains are a refuge for the stags and the rock for the rabbits.

He appointed the moon for seasons: the sun knows his going down.

You made darkness and it was night; in it all the wild beasts of the forest creep forth:

Even young lions roaring for [their] prey and to seek meat for themselves from God.

The sun arises and they shall be gathered together, they shall lie down in their dens.

Man shall go forth to his work and to his labor until the evening.

How great are your works, O Lord! in wisdom have you have made them all: the earth is filled with your creation.

So is this great and wide sea: there are things creeping innumerable, animals both small and great.

There go the ships; and this dragon you have made to play in it.

All wait upon you, to give them their food in due season.

When you have given it to them, they will gather it; when you have opened your hand, they shall all be filled with good.

But when you have turned away your face, they shall be troubled: you will take away their breath; they shall fail and return to their dust.

You shall send forth your Spirit and they shall be created; and you shall renew the face of the earth.

Let the glory of the Lord be for ever: the Lord shall rejoice in his works;

Who looks upon the earth and makes it tremble; who touches the mountains and they smoke.

I will sing to the Lord while I live; I will sing praise to my God while I have being.

Let my meditation be sweet to him: I will rejoice in the Lord!

Let the sinners vanish from the earth, and transgressors, that they shall be no more. Bless the Lord, O my soul!

And again.

The sun knows his going down. You made darkness and it was night.

How great are your works, O Lord! in wisdom have you have made them all: the earth is filled with your creation.

Glory to the Father and the Son and the Holy Spirit. Both now and ever, and to the ages of ages. Amen.

Alleluia, Alleluia, Alleluia. Glory to you, O God. *(x3) (After the third)* Our hope, O Lord, Glory to you.

Psalm 140

Lord, I have cried unto You; hear me. Hear me, O Lord. Lord, I have cried unto you; hear me. Attend to the voice of my supplication when I cry unto You; hear me, O Lord.

Let my prayer be set forth as incense before You, the lifting up of my hands as the evening sacrifice; hear me, O Lord.

Set a watch, O Lord, before my mouth and a protecting door about my lips.

Incline not my heart to evil words to make excuses in sins.

With those who work iniquity; and I will not associate with the choicest of them.

Let the righteous man chasten me with mercy and reprove me; as for the oil of the sinner, let it not anoint my head.

For even my prayer is against their good pleasure. Their judges have been swallowed up like a rock.

They shall hear my words, for they are sweet. As a clod of earth is broken on the ground, so their bones are scattered by the side of Hades.

For to You, O Lord, O Lord, are my eyes; I have hoped in You; take not away my soul.

Keep me from the snare which they have laid for me, and from the stumbling blocks of those who work iniquity.

The sinners shall fall into their own net. I am apart from them until I pass away.

Psalm 141

With my voice, to the Lord have I cried; with my voice, to the Lord have I made my supplication.

I shall pour out before Him my supplication; my affliction before Him shall I declare,

As my spirit is departing from within me; and You knew my paths.

In this way on which I was walking they hid a snare for me.

I looked to my right and beheld, and there was no one that knew me.

There is no escape for me, and no one searching for my soul.

I cried to You, O Lord; I said: You are my hope, You are my portion in the land of the living.

Attend to my supplication; for I have been greatly humbled.

Deliver me from those who pursue me, for they have become stronger than I.

From here the appointed hymns as indicated in the Typikon are chanted in alternation with the final verses, according to the number of hymns.

Verse. Bring my soul out of prison, that I may confess your name.

Verse. The just will await me, until you reward me.

Verse. Out of the depths I have cried to you, O Lord. Lord hear my voice.

Verse. Let your ears be attentive, to the voice of my supplication.

Verse. If you, Lord, should mark iniquities, Lord, who will stand? But there is forgiveness with you.

Verse. For your name's sake I have waited for you, O Lord. My soul has waited on your word. My soul has hoped in the Lord.

Verse. From the morning watch until night, from the morning watch, let Israel hope in the Lord.

Verse. For with the Lord there is mercy, and with him plentiful redemption, and he will redeem Israel from all his iniquities.

Verse. Praise the Lord, all you nations. Praise him all you peoples.

Verse. For his mercy has been mighty towards us, and the truth of the Lord endures to the ages.

Glory to the Father and to the Son and to the Holy Spirit.

Doxasticon.

Both now and forever, and to the ages of ages. Amen.

Theotokion.

O joyful Light of the holy glory of the immortal, heavenly, holy, blessed Father, O Jesus Christ. Now that we have come to the setting of the sun and see the evening light, we sing the praise of God, Father, Son and Holy Spirit. It is right at all times to hymn you with holy voices, Son of God, giver of life. Therefore the world glorifies you.

PROKEIMENA

Saturday Evening. Tone Pl. 2.

The Lord has reigned; He has clothed himself with majesty.

Verse 1. The Lord has put on power and girded himself.

Verse 2. For He has established the universe, which shall not be shaken.

Sunday Evening. Tone Pl. 4.

Behold, now bless the Lord, all you servants of the Lord.

Verse. You that stand in the house of the Lord, in the courts of the House of our God.

Monday Evening. Tone 4.

The Lord will hear me, when I cry out to Him.

Verse. When I called, You heard me, O God of my righteousness. In affliction, You extended me.

Tuesday Evening. Tone 1.

Your mercy will pursue me, O Lord, all the days of my life.

Verse. The Lord is my shepherd, and I will lack nothing; He settled me in a place of green pasture.

Wednesday Evening. Tone Pl. 1.

O God, in Your name save me, and in Your power You will judge me.

Verse. O God, hear my prayer, give ear to the words of my mouth.

Thursday Evening. Tone Pl. 2.

My help is from the Lord, who made heaven and the earth.

Verse. I lifted up my eyes to the mountains, from where my help will come.

Friday Evening. Tone Varys.

O God, You are my helper; Your mercy will go before me.

Verse. Deliver me from my enemies, O God, deliver me from those who rise up against me.

The readings follow if any.

Grant, Lord, to keep us this evening without sin. Blessed are you, Lord, the God of our fathers, and praised and glorified is your name to the ages. Amen. Let your mercy, Lord be upon us, as we have hoped in you. Blessed are you, Lord: teach me your statutes. Blessed are you, Master: make me understand your statutes. Blessed are you, Holy One: enlighten me with your statutes. Lord, your mercy is for ever; do not scorn the work of your hands. To you praise is due, to you song is due, to you glory is due, to the Father, and to the Son, and to the Holy Spirit, now and for ever, and to the ages of ages. Amen.

Prayer of Symeon the God Receiver

Now, Master, you let your servant depart in peace, according to your word; for my eyes have seen your Salvation, which you have prepared before the face of all peoples, a Light to bring revelation to the nations, and the Glory of your people Israel.

Holy God, Holy Mighty, Holy Immortal, have mercy on us. (x3)

Glory to the Father, and the Son, and the Holy Spirit, now and forever and to the ages of ages. Amen.

All-holy Trinity, have mercy on us. Lord, forgive our sins. Master, pardon our transgressions. Holy One, visit and heal our infirmities for the glory of Your name.

Lord, have mercy. (x3) Glory to the Father, and the Son, and the Holy Spirit, now and forever and to the ages of ages. Amen.

Our Father, who art in heaven, hallowed be Thy name. Thy kingdom come. Thy will be done, on earth as it is in heaven. Give us this day our daily bread; and forgive us our trespasses, as we forgive those who trespass against us. And lead us not into temptation, but deliver us from the evil one.

Through the prayers of our Holy Fathers, Lord Jesus Christ our God, have mercy upon us and save us. Amen.

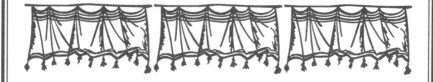

SMALL COMPLINE

This service is read directly after the evening meal.

In the name of the Father and the Son and the Holy Spirit, now and forever and the ages of ages. Amen.

Glory to you, our God, glory to you.

Heavenly King, comforter, the Spirit of truth, who are present everywhere filling all things, Treasury of good things and Giver of life, come and dwell in us, Cleanse us of every stain, and save our souls, gracious Lord.

Holy God, Holy Mighty, Holy Immortal, have mercy on us. *(x3)*

Glory to the Father, and the Son, and the Holy Spirit, now and forever and to the ages of ages. Amen.

All-holy Trinity, have mercy on us. Lord, forgive our sins. Master, pardon our transgressions. Holy One, visit and heal our infirmities for the glory of Your name.

Lord, have mercy. *(x3)* Glory to the Father, and the Son, and the Holy Spirit, now and forever and to the ages of ages. Amen.

Our Father, who art in heaven, hallowed be Thy name. Thy kingdom come. Thy will be done, on earth as it is in heaven. Give us this day our daily bread; and forgive us our trespasses, as we forgive those who trespass against us. And lead us not into temptation, but deliver us from the evil one.

Through the prayers of our Holy Fathers, Lord Jesus Christ our God, have mercy upon us and save us. Amen.

Psalm 50

Have mercy upon me, O God, according to your great mercy; according to the multitude of your compassions blot out my transgression.

Wash me thoroughly from my iniquity and cleanse me from my sin.

For I am conscious of my iniquity; and my sin is continually before me.

Against you alone have I sinned and done evil before you: that you might be justified in your sayings and overcome in your judgments.

For, behold, I was conceived in iniquities and in sins did my mother conceive me.

For, behold, you love truth: you have manifested to me the secret and hidden things of your wisdom.

You shall sprinkle me with hyssop and I shall be purified: you shall wash me and I shall be made whiter than snow.

You shall cause me to hear gladness and joy: the afflicted bones shall rejoice.

Turn away your face from my sins and blot out all my iniquities.

Create in me a clean heart, O God; and renew a right spirit in my inner being.

Do not cast me away from your presence; and do not remove your holy Spirit from me.

Restore to me the joy of your salvation: establish me with your guiding Spirit.

Then will I teach transgressors your ways; and ungodly men shall return to you.

Deliver me from blood guiltiness, O God, the God of my salvation: then my tongue shall joyfully declare your righteousness.

O Lord, you shall open my lips; and my mouth shall declare your praise.

If you desired sacrifice, I would have given it: you will not take pleasure in whole-burnt-offerings.

Sacrifice to God is a broken spirit: a broken and humbled heart God will not despise.

Do good, O Lord, to Zion in your good pleasure; Let the walls of Jerusalem be rebuilt.

Then shall you be pleased with a sacrifice of righteousness, with offering and whole-burnt sacrifices: then shall they offer calves upon your altar.

Psalm 69

Draw near, O God, to my help.

Let them be ashamed and confounded that seek my soul: let them be turned backward and put to shame, those who wish me evil.

Let those who say to me, Aha, aha, be turned back and put to shame at once.

Let all who seek you exult and be glad in you: Let those who love your salvation say continually, Let God be magnified!

But I am poor and needy; O God, help me: you are my helper and deliverer; O Lord, do not delay.

Psalm 142

O Lord, attend to my prayer: hearken to my supplication in your truth; hear me in your righteousness.

Do not enter into judgment with your servant, for in your sight shall no man living be justified.

For the enemy has persecuted my soul; he has brought my life down to the ground; he has made me to dwell in a dark place, as those who have been long dead.

Therefore my spirit was grieved in me; my heart was troubled within me.

I remembered the days of old; and I meditated on all your doings: yes, I meditated on the works of your hands.

I spread forth my hands to you; my soul thirsts for you, as a dry land.

Hear me speedily, O Lord; my spirit has failed; turn not away your face from me, else I shall be like to those who go down to the pit.

Cause me to hear your mercy in the morning; for I have hoped in you; make known to me, O Lord, the way by which I should walk; for I have lifted up my soul to you.

Deliver me from my enemies, O Lord; for I have fled to you for refuge.

Teach me to do your will; for you are my God; your good Spirit shall guide me in the straight way.

You shall revive me, O Lord, for your name's sake; in your righteousness you shall bring my soul out of affliction.

In your mercy you will destroy my enemies and destroy all those who afflict my soul, for I am your servant.

DOXOLOGY
Small

Glory to God in the highest, and on earth peace, goodwill among men.

We praise you, we bless you, we worship you, we glorify you, we give you thanks for your great glory.

Lord, King, God of heaven, Father almighty: Lord, only-begotten Son, Jesus Christ and Holy Spirit.

Lord God, Lamb of God, Son of the Father, who take away the sin of the world, have mercy on us; you take away the sins of the world.

Receive our prayer, you who sit on the right hand of the Father, and have mercy on us.

For you alone are holy, you alone are Lord, Jesus Christ, to the glory of God the Father. Amen.

Every day I will bless you, and praise your name for ever and to the ages of ages.

Lord, you have been our refuge from generation to generation. I said, Lord, have mercy on me, heal my soul, for I have sinned against you.

Lord, I have run to you for refuge: teach me to do your will, for you are my God.

For with you is the source of life: and in your light we shall see light. Continue your mercy towards those who know you. Grant, Lord, this day to keep us without sin.

Blessed are you, O Lord, the God of our fathers, and praised and glorified is your name to the ages. Amen.

May your mercy, O Lord, be upon us, as we have put our hope in you.

Blessed are you, Lord, teach me your statutes. Blessed are you, Master, make me understand your statutes. Blessed are you, Holy One, enlighten me with your statutes.

Lord, your mercy is for ever; do not scorn the work of your hands.

To you praise is due, to you song is due, to you glory is due, Father, Son and Holy Spirit, now and for ever, and to the ages of ages. Amen.

THE SYMBOL OF FAITH

I believe in one God, Father Almighty, Creator of heaven and earth and of all things visible and invisible.

And in one Lord Jesus Christ, the only-begotten Son of God, begotten of the Father before all ages. Light of Light, true God of true God, begotten not created, of one essence with the Father through Whom all things were made.

Who for us men and for our salvation came down from heaven and was incarnate of the Holy Spirit and the Virgin Mary and became man.

He was crucified for us under Pontius Pilate. He suffered and was buried.

And He rose on the third day, according to the Scriptures.

He ascended into heaven and is seated at the right hand of the Father.

And He will come again with glory to judge the living and dead. His kingdom shall have no end.

And in the Holy Spirit, the Lord, the Creator of life, Who proceeds from the Father, Who together with the Father and the Son is worshiped and glorified, Who spoke through the prophets.

In one, holy, catholic, and apostolic Church.

I confess one baptism for the forgiveness of sins.

I look for the resurrection of the dead and the life of the age to come. Amen.

If you intend to approach the most pure Mysteries on the following day, it is customary to read the Canon of Preparation at this point, see pg. 175.

It is truly right to call you blest, O Theotokos, the ever blessed, you who are most pure and the Mother of our God.

Greater in honor than the Cherubim, and beyond compare more glorious than the Seraphim, without corruption you gave birth to God the Word, truly the Mother of God we magnify you.

Holy God, Holy Mighty, Holy Immortal, have mercy on us. *(x3)*

Glory to the Father, and the Son, and the Holy Spirit, now and forever and to the ages of ages. Amen.

All-holy Trinity, have mercy on us. Lord, forgive our sins. Master, pardon our transgressions. Holy One, visit and heal our infirmities for the glory of Your name.

Lord, have mercy. *(x3)* Glory to the Father, and the Son, and the Holy Spirit, now and forever and to the ages of ages. Amen.

Our Father, who art in heaven, hallowed be Thy name. Thy kingdom come. Thy will be done, on earth as it is in heaven. Give us this day our daily bread; and forgive us our trespasses, as we forgive those who trespass against us. And lead us not into temptation, but deliver us from the evil one.

Through the prayers of our Holy Fathers, Lord Jesus Christ our God, have mercy upon us and save us. Amen.

God of our fathers, who always deal with us in your forbearance, do not withdraw your pity from us, but at the intercessions of our fathers, guide our life in peace.

Your Church, clothed throughout the world as in purple and fine linen with the blood of your Martyrs, cries out to you through them: Christ, our God, send down your mercy on your people; give peace to your city and to our souls your great mercy.

Glory to the Father and to the Son and to the Holy Spirit.

With the Saints, O Christ, give rest to the souls of your servants, where there is neither sickness, nor sorrow, nor sighing, but life without end.

Both now and for ever, and to the ages of ages. Amen.

Through the intercession of all the Saints and of the Mother of God, give us your peace, Lord, and have mercy on us, for you alone are merciful.

Lord, have mercy *(x40)*.

At every time and at every hour, in heaven and on earth worshiped and glorified, Christ God, long-suffering, great in mercy, great in compassion, loving the just and merciful to sinners, calling all to salvation by the promise of the good things to come; do you, Lord, yourself accept our entreaties at this hour, and direct our lives to your commandments. Sanctify our souls, purify our bodies, correct our thoughts, cleanse our ideas and deliver us from every distress, evil, and pain. Wall us about with your holy Angels, that protected and guided by their host we may reach the unity of the faith and the knowledge of your unapproachable glory; for you are blessed to the ages of ages. Amen.

Lord, have mercy. *(x3)*

Glory to the Father and to the Son and to the Holy Spirit, now and forever and to the ages of ages. Amen.

Greater in honor than the Cherubim, and beyond compare more glorious than the Seraphim, without corruption you gave birth to God the Word, truly the Mother of God we magnify you.

Through the prayers of our Holy Fathers, Lord Jesus Christ our God, have mercy and save us. Amen.

Lord, have mercy. *(x3)*

And save and help us, All-holy Virgin.

Prayer to the Most Holy Theotokos

by Paul, monk of the Monastery of Evergetis.

O spotless, undefiled, incorrupt, immaculate, pure Virgin, Lady Bride of God, who by your extraordinary conceiving united God the Word to humanity and joined the outcast nature of our race to the things in heaven; O only hope of the hopeless, and help of the beleaguered; the ready assistance of them that run to you, and refuge of all Christians: Abhor me not the abominable sinner, who with depraved thoughts and words and acts have rendered myself altogether worthless, and have willfully become a slave to the languor of the pleasures of this life. But rather, as the Mother of the God who loves mankind, in your own loving care for mankind, take pity on me the sinner and prodigal, and accept this supplication of mine offered to you from sordid lips. And employing your motherly candor, entreat your Son, our Master and Lord, that He open His humane and benevolent heart to me, and that, overlooking my innumerable faults, He convert me to repentance and make me a proficient worker of His commandments. And inasmuch as you are merciful, sympathetic and charitable, ever be with me: in this life, as a fervent protectress and helper, blocking the assaults of the adversaries and guiding me to salvation; and in the hour of my departure, escorting my wretched soul, driving far from it the dark visages of the evil demons; while on the dread day of judgement, delivering me from eternal torment, and making me an heir of the ineffable glory of your Son and our God. Which glory may I attain, O my Lady, most-holy Theotokos, through your mediation and assistance, by the grace and the love for mankind of your only-begotten Son, our Lord and God and Savior Jesus Christ, to whom is due all glory, honor and worship, together with His unoriginate Father and His all-holy, good and life-giving Spirit, now and forever, and to the ages of ages. Amen.

Prayer to Our Lord Jesus Christ

by the monk Antiochus of Pandektos.

And grant us, O Master, as we retire for sleep, rest of body and soul. And keep us from the murky sleep of sin and from every dark pleasure of the night. Halt the drives of the passions, extinguish the fiery darts that the evil one cunningly throws at us. Arrest the insurrections of our flesh, and still our every earthly and material way of thought. And grant us, O God, a wakeful mind, prudent thought, a watchful heart, and sleep that is light and free of any satanic fantasy. And rouse us at the hour of prayer, confirmed in Your commandments, and holding in ourselves the unbroken memory of Your judgments. Grant that we may sing Your glory all the night long, and so hymn and bless and glorify Your all-honored and majestic name, of the Father and the Son and the Holy Spirit, now and forever, and to the ages of ages. Amen.

Most glorious, ever-virgin, blessed Theotokos, present our prayer to your Son and our God, and ask that through you He save our souls.

Prayer of Saint Ioannikios

My hope is the Father, my refuge is the Son, my shelter is the Holy Spirit. O Holy Trinity, glory to You.

O Mother of God, I have committed my every hope wholly unto you. Keep me under your shelter.

Holy Angel, attendant on my wretched soul and my afflicted life, forsake me not, a sinner, nor depart from me because of my lack of self-control. Give no place to the wicked demon to dominate me through prevailing over this mortal body of mine. Hold my wretched and feeble hand, and lead me on the way of salvation. Yes, O holy Angel of God, the guardian and protector of my wretched soul and body, forgive me everything that I have done to trouble you all the days of my life, and if I have sinned in anything today. Shelter me tonight, and preserve me from every prank of the enemy, that I not anger God by any sin. And intercede with the Lord on my behalf, that He strengthen me in the fear of Him, and that He make me a worthy servant of His goodness. Amen.

Virgin Theotokos, Rejoice Mary full of grace, the Lord is with you. Blessed are you among women, and blessed is the fruit of your womb, for you have given birth to the Saviour of our souls.

To you my Champion and Commander, I your city saved from disasters dedicate, O Mother of God, hymns of victory and thanksgiving; but as you have unassailable might from every kind of danger now deliver me, that I may cry to you: Rejoice, Bride without bridegroom!

Most Holy Theotokos, save us.

Virgin Theotokos, Rejoice Mary full of grace, the Lord is with you. Blessed are you among women, and blessed is the fruit of your womb, for you have given birth to the Saviour of our souls. (*x3*)

Through the prayers of our Holy Fathers, Lord Jesus Christ our God, have mercy and save us. Amen.

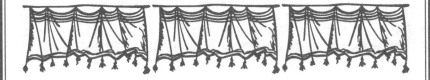

The Queen of All

THE SALUTATIONS
TO THE MOST HOLY
THEOTOKOS

The Akathist Hymn.

When the bodiless one learned the secret command, in haste he came and stood before Joseph's dwelling, and spoke unto the Maiden who knew not wedlock: The One who bowed the Heavens by His decent is held and contained unchanging wholly in you. Seeing Him receiving the form of a servant in your womb, I stand in awe and cry to you: Rejoice, Bride without bridegroom.

To you my Champion and Commander, I your city saved from disasters dedicate, O Mother of God, hymns of victory and thanksgiving; but as you have unassailable might from every kind of danger now deliver me, that I may cry to you: Rejoice, Bride without bridegroom!

Section 1. The Annunciation

1kos 1

A prince of the angels was sent from heaven, to say to the Mother of God, 'Rejoice!' *(x3)* And as, at his bodiless voice, he saw you, Lord, embodied, he was astounded and stood still, crying out to her like this:

Rejoice, you through whom joy will shine out, Rejoice, you through whom the curse will cease.

Rejoice, recalling of fallen Adam, Rejoice, redemption of the tears of Eve.

Rejoice, height hard to climb for human thoughts, Rejoice, depth hard to scan even for angels' eyes.

Rejoice, for you are a throne for the King, Rejoice, for you carry the One who carries all.

Rejoice, star that makes visible the Sun, Rejoice, womb of divine incarnation.

Rejoice, you through whom creation is renewed. Rejoice, you through whom the Creator becomes a babe.

Rejoice, Bride without bridegroom.

Kontakion 1

But the holy Virgin, seeing herself pure, says boldly to Gabriel, 'The strangeness of your words seems hard for my soul to accept. For from a conception without seed you foretell pregnancy, as you cry: Alleluia!'

Ikos 2

Calling to the ministering angel, the Virgin sought to know unknown knowledge, 'From a pure womb how can a son be born? Tell me.' He spoke to her in fear, only crying out:

Rejoice, initiate of an ineffable counsel, Rejoice, faith in things that demand silence.

Rejoice, beginning of Christ's wonders, Rejoice, crown of his teachings.

Rejoice, heavenly ladder by which God came down, Rejoice, bridge, leading those from earth to heaven.

Rejoice, wonder well-known among the angels, Rejoice, wound much lamented by the demons.

Rejoice, for ineffably you gave birth to the Light, Rejoice, for to none you revealed the mystery.

Rejoice, you that surpass the knowledge of the wise, Rejoice, you that pour light on the minds of believers.

Rejoice, Bride without bridegroom.

Kontakion 2

Divine power of the Most High then overshadowed for conception the one who knew not wedlock. And he made her womb fruitful as a fertile field for all who wish to reap salvation as they sing: Alleluia!

Ikos 3

Enclosing God within her womb, the Virgin hastened to Elizabeth; whose infant at once recognized her greeting, and rejoicing with leaps as though with songs, cried out to the Mother of God:

Rejoice, vine with a branch that does not wither, Rejoice, orchard of fruit that bears no taint.

Rejoice, for you husband the Husbandman who loves mankind, Rejoice, for you cultivate the Cultivator of our life.

Rejoice, ploughland yielding a rich harvest of compassion, Rejoice, table laden with abundance of mercy.

Rejoice, for you make the meadow of delight flower again, Rejoice, for you make ready a haven for the soul.

Rejoice, acceptable incense of intercession, Rejoice, propitiation for the whole world.

Rejoice, good pleasure of God towards mortals, Rejoice, freedom of speech of mortals towards God.

Rejoice, Bride without bridegroom.

Kontakion 3

Feeling in himself a storm of doubtful thoughts, prudent Joseph was troubled, seeing that you were unwedded, and he suspected a stolen union, blameless Maiden. But when he learnt that your conceiving was from the Holy Spirit, he said: Alleluia!

Section 2. On the Nativity

Ikos 4

God's coming in the flesh the Shepherds heard the angels praising. And hastening as to a shepherd, they see him as a spotless lamb being pastured in the womb of Mary. Praising her they said:

Rejoice, mother of the lamb and shepherd, Rejoice, fold of spiritual sheep.

Rejoice, defense against unseen foes. Rejoice, key that opens the doors of Paradise.

Rejoice, for things in heaven exult with earth, Rejoice, for things on earth rejoice with heaven.

Rejoice, never-silent voice of the Apostles, Rejoice, never-conquered courage of the Champions.

Rejoice, firm foundation of the Faith, Rejoice, shining revelation of Grace.

Rejoice, you through whom Hell was stripped bare, Rejoice, you through whom we were clothed with glory.

Rejoice, Bride without bridegroom.

Kontakion 4

Having seen a star leading to God, Magi followed its radiance. Holding to it as a beacon, through it they searched for a mighty king. And having attained the Unattainable they rejoiced and cried to him: Alleluia!

Ikos 5

In the hands of the Virgin children of the Chaldeans saw the one who with his hands fashioned humankind. And knowing him to be their Master, though he had taken the form of a servant, they hastened to honor him with their gifts and to cry to the Blessed Maiden:

Rejoice, mother of the star that never sets, Rejoice, radiance of the mystical day.

Rejoice, for you quenched the furnace of deception, Rejoice, for you enlighten the initiates of the Trinity.

Rejoice, for you cast out from his rule the inhuman tyrant, Rejoice, for you revealed Christ, the Lord who loves humankind.

Rejoice, deliverance from pagan worship, Rejoice, liberation from filthy deeds.

Rejoice, for you ended the worship of fire, Rejoice, for you deliver from the flame of passions.

Rejoice, guide of believers to chastity, Rejoice, joy of all generations.

Rejoice, Bride without bridegroom.

Kontakion 5

Journeying back to Babylon, for they had fulfilled the prophecy concerning you, the Magi, become God-bearing heralds, proclaimed you to all as Christ, leaving Herod like an idiot who did not know how to sing: Alleluia!

Ikos 6

Kindling in Egypt the light of truth, you dispelled the darkness of falsehood. For its idols, O Saviour, not able to withstand your strength, fell down, while those who were delivered from them cried out to the Mother of God:

Rejoice, restoration of humans, Rejoice, downfall of the demons.

Rejoice, for you trampled on the error of deception, Rejoice, for you exposed the trickery of idols.

Rejoice, sea that drowned the Pharaoh of the mind, Rejoice, rock that gave drink to those thirsting for life.

Rejoice, pillar of fire, guiding those in darkness, Rejoice, protection of the world, wider than the cloud.

Rejoice, food that replaced the manna, Rejoice, minister of holy delight.

Rejoice, Bride without bridegroom.

Kontakion 6

When Symeon was about to depart from this present age of deception, you were given to him as a babe, but you were known to him also as perfect God. And so, struck with amazement at your ineffable wisdom, he cried: Alleluia!

Section 3. On the Incarnation

Ikos 7

Manifesting himself to us, who came into being by him, the Creator revealed a new creation, for he budded from a womb without seed and preserved it as it was, incorrupt, that seeing the wonder we might sing her praises crying:

Rejoice, flower of incorruption, Rejoice, crown of self-mastery.

Rejoice, for you show a bright image of the resurrection, Rejoice, for you reveal the angels' way of life.

Rejoice, tree of glorious fruit from which believers are nourished, Rejoice, wood with shady leaves under which many shelter.

Rejoice, for you conceived a guide for those gone astray, Rejoice, for you bore a deliverer for captives.

Rejoice, intercessor with the just Judge, Rejoice, forgiveness for many who stumble.

Rejoice, robe for those stripped of freedom of speech, Rejoice, love that conquers every longing.

Rejoice, Bride without bridegroom.

Kontakion 7

Now that we have seen a strange birth, let us become strangers to the world, fixing our minds in heaven. For this the most high God appeared on earth as a lowly human, wishing to draw on high those who cry out to him: Alleluia!

Ikos 8

The uncircumscribed Word was wholly present among things below and in no way absent from those on high. For it was God's condescension, and not a change of place, and birth from a Virgin filled by God, who hears these words:

Rejoice, enclosure of God who cannot be enclosed, Rejoice, door of a hallowed mystery.

Rejoice, doubtful tidings for unbelievers, Rejoice, undoubted boast for all believers.

Rejoice, all-holy chariot of him who rides upon the Cherubim, Rejoice, best of dwellings of him who is above the Seraphim.

Rejoice, for you bring opposites to harmony, Rejoice, for you yoke child-birth and virginity.

Rejoice, for through you transgression has been abolished, Rejoice, for through you Paradise has been opened.

Rejoice, key of Christ's kingdom, Rejoice, hope of eternal blessings.

Rejoice, Bride without bridegroom.

Kontakion 8

Every angelic being was amazed at the great work of your incarnation. For they saw the One who is Unapproachable as God, as a mortal approachable by all, living his life among us, while hearing from us all: Alleluia!

Ikos 9

Eloquent orators we see dumb as fishes before you, Theotokos. For they are at a loss to say how you remain Virgin, yet are able to give birth! But we, marveling at the mystery, cry out with faith:

Rejoice, vessel of the wisdom of God. Rejoice, storehouse of his providence.

Rejoice, who show lovers of wisdom to be without wisdom. Rejoice, who prove those skilled in reasoning —to be without reason.

Rejoice, because subtle seekers have been made fools. Rejoice, because myth makers have been made to wither.

Rejoice, who tear apart the webs of the Athenians. Rejoice, who fill full the nets of the Fishermen.

Rejoice, who draw up from the depths of ignorance. Rejoice, who enlighten many with knowledge.

Rejoice, boat for those who want to be saved. Rejoice, harbor for the seafarers of life.

Rejoice, Bride without bridegroom!

Kontakion 9

Wishing to save the world, the One who orders all things came to it of his own free will. And as God, being shepherd, for our sake he appeared as a man like us. For having called like to Like, as God he hears: Alleluia!

Ikos 10

You are a wall for virgins, Virgin Mother of God, and for all who have recourse to you. For the Maker of heaven and earth made you ready, O most pure, dwelling in your womb and teaching all to call to you:

Rejoice, pillar of virginity. Rejoice, gate of salvation.

Rejoice, source of spiritual refashioning. Rejoice, giver of divine loving kindness.

Rejoice, for you gave new birth to those conceived in shame. Rejoice, for you gave counsel to those robbed of understanding.

Rejoice, who destroy the corrupter of minds. Rejoice, who gave birth to the sower of purity.

Rejoice, bridal chamber of a marriage without seed. Rejoice, who unite believers to the Lord.

Rejoice, fair nursemaid of virgins. Rejoice, bridesmaid of holy souls:

Rejoice, Bride without bridegroom!

Kontakion 10

Every hymn fails that seeks to match the multitude of your many mercies. For even if we offer you, O holy King, songs equal in number to the sand, we achieve nothing worthy of what you have given us, who cry to you: Alleluia!

Ikos 11

We see the holy Virgin as a lamp that bears the light, shining for those in darkness. For kindling the immaterial Light she guides all to divine knowledge, enlightening the mind by its ray, honored with this cry:

Rejoice, beam of the immaterial sun, Rejoice, ray of the moon that never sets.

Rejoice, lightning flash that shines on souls. Rejoice, thunder that terrifies the foe.

Rejoice, for you make the enlightenment with many lights to dawn. Rejoice, for you make the river with many streams to flow.

Rejoice, who prefigure the baptismal font. Rejoice, who take away the filth of sin.

Rejoice, bath that washes clean the conscience. Rejoice, bowl in which the wine of joy is mixed.

Rejoice, scent of Christ's fragrance. Rejoice, life of mystical feasting.

Rejoice, Bride without bridegroom!

Kontakion 11

Wishing to give release from ancient offenses, the Creditor of all humanity came of himself to those who were exiled from his grace, and having torn up their bond he hears from all as follows: Alleluia.

Ikos 12

Your Offspring we sing and all raise to you our hymn as a living temple, Mother of God. For having dwelt in your womb, the Lord who holds all things in his hand sanctified, glorified and taught all to cry out to you:

Rejoice, tabernacle of God the Word, Rejoice, greater Holy of Holies.

Rejoice, Ark gilded by the Spirit, Rejoice, inexhaustible treasure of life.

Rejoice, precious diadem of Orthodox kings, Rejoice, honored boast of devout priests.

Rejoice, unshakeable tower of the Church, Rejoice, unbreachable wall of the Kingdom.

Rejoice, through whom trophies are raised, Rejoice, through whom enemies fall.

Rejoice, healing of my flesh, Rejoice, salvation of my soul.

Rejoice, Bride without bridegroom!

Kontakion 12

O Mother, all praised, who gave birth to the Word, the Holiest of all Holies, (x3) accepting our present offering, deliver us all from every disaster and rescue from the punishment to come those who cry out together, Alleluia.

A prince of the angels was sent from heaven, to say to the Mother of God, 'Rejoice!' *(x3)* And as, at his bodiless voice, he saw you, Lord, embodied, he was astounded and stood still, crying out to her like this:

Rejoice, you through whom joy will shine out, Rejoice, you through whom the curse will cease.

Rejoice, recalling of fallen Adam, Rejoice, redemption of the tears of Eve.

Rejoice, height hard to climb for human thoughts, Rejoice, depth hard to scan even for angels' eyes.

Rejoice, for you are a throne for the King, Rejoice, for you carry the One who carries all.

Rejoice, star that makes visible the Sun, Rejoice, womb of divine incarnation.

Rejoice, you through whom creation is renewed. Rejoice, you through whom the Creator becomes a babe.

Rejoice, Bride without bridegroom!

To you my Champion and Commander, I your city saved from disasters dedicate, O Mother of God, hymns of victory and thanksgiving; but as you have unassailable might from every kind of danger now deliver me, that I may cry to you: Rejoice, Bride without bridegroom!

Rejoice, Bride without bridegroom!

Our Merciful Mother of Kykkos

THE SERVICE OF THE SMALL PARAKLESIS TO THE MOST HOLY THEOTOKOS

A POEM OF THEOSTIRIKTOS THE MONK

The Small Supplicatory Canon is sung for any need, and in affliction of soul, as well as during the first fifteen days of August, alternating between it and the Great Supplicatory Canon.

Heavenly King, comforter, the Spirit of truth, who are present everywhere filling all things, Treasury of good things and Giver of life, come and dwell in us, Cleanse us of every stain, and save our souls, gracious Lord.

Holy God, Holy Mighty, Holy Immortal, have mercy on us. (*x3*)

Glory to the Father, and the Son, and the Holy Spirit, now and forever and to the ages of ages. Amen.

All-holy Trinity, have mercy on us. Lord, forgive our sins. Master, pardon our transgressions. Holy One, visit and heal our infirmities for the glory of Your name.

Lord, have mercy. (*x3*) Glory to the Father, and the Son, and the Holy Spirit, now and forever and to the ages of ages. Amen.

Our Father, who art in heaven, hallowed be Thy name. Thy kingdom come. Thy will be done, on earth as it is in heaven. Give us this day our daily bread; and forgive us our trespasses, as we forgive those who trespass against us. And lead us not into temptation, but deliver us from the evil one.

Through the prayers of our Holy Fathers, Lord Jesus Christ our God, have mercy upon us and save us. Amen.

Psalm 142

O Lord, attend to my prayer: hearken to my supplication in your truth; hear me in your righteousness.

Do not enter into judgment with your servant, for in your sight shall no man living be justified.

For the enemy has persecuted my soul; he has brought my life down to the ground; he has made me to dwell in a dark place, as those who have been long dead.

Therefore my spirit was grieved in me; my heart was troubled within me.

I remembered the days of old; and I meditated on all your doings: yes, I meditated on the works of your hands.

I spread forth my hands to you; my soul thirsts for you, as a dry land.

Hear me speedily, O Lord; my spirit has failed; turn not away your face from me, else I shall be like to those who go down to the pit.

Cause me to hear your mercy in the morning; for I have hoped in you; make known to me, O Lord, the way by which I should walk; for I have lifted up my soul to you.

Deliver me from my enemies, O Lord; for I have fled to you for refuge.

Teach me to do your will; for you are my God; your good Spirit shall guide me in the straight way.

You shall revive me, O Lord, for your name's sake; in your righteousness you shall bring my soul out of affliction.

In your mercy you will destroy my enemies and destroy all those who afflict my soul, for I am your servant.

And immediately the choirs sing God is the Lord *antiphonally, as follows:*

Psalm 117

Tone 4.

God is the Lord, and He appeared to us. Blessed is He who comes in the name of the Lord.

Verse 1: *Give thanks to the Lord and call upon His holy name.*

God is the Lord, and He appeared to us. Blessed is He who comes in the name of the Lord.

Verse 2: *All the nations surrounded me, but in the name of the Lord I defended myself against them.*

God is the Lord, and He appeared to us. Blessed is He who comes in the name of the Lord.

Verse 3: *This came about from the Lord, and it is wonderful in our eyes.*

God is the Lord, and He appeared to us. Blessed is He who comes in the name of the Lord.

Then the following:

Troparia.

Tone 4. *Lifted up on the Cross.*

Now to the Theotokos let us humble sinners run in haste * and in repentance let us fall down before her feet, * crying aloud with fervor from the depths of our souls, * 'Sovereign Lady, help us now, * have compassion upon us, * hasten, for we perish * from our many offenses. * Let not your servants go empty away; * we have you as our only hope'.

Glory to the Father, and the Son and the Holy Spirit.

The same, or the Apolytikion of the Church.

Both now and forever and to the ages of ages. Amen.

Though most unworthy, may we never by silence * fail to proclaim your mighty acts and accomplishments, * for if you do not stand to intercede for us all, * Theotokos, who then * will preserve us in freedom? * Who would have delivered us * from such terrible dangers? * O Sovereign Lady, from all kinds of threats * you save your servants, * may we not abandon you.

Psalm 50

Have mercy upon me, O God, according to your great mercy; according to the multitude of your compassions blot out my transgression.

Wash me thoroughly from my iniquity and cleanse me from my sin.

For I am conscious of my iniquity; and my sin is continually before me.

Against you alone have I sinned and done evil before you: that you might be justified in your sayings and overcome in your judgments.

For, behold, I was conceived in iniquities and in sins did my mother conceive me.

For, behold, you love truth: you have manifested to me the secret and hidden things of your wisdom.

You shall sprinkle me with hyssop and I shall be purified: you shall wash me and I shall be made whiter than snow.

You shall cause me to hear gladness and joy: the afflicted bones shall rejoice.

Turn away your face from my sins and blot out all my iniquities.

Create in me a clean heart, O God; and renew a right spirit in my inner being.

Do not cast me away from your presence; and do not remove your holy Spirit from me.

Restore to me the joy of your salvation: establish me with your guiding Spirit.

Then will I teach transgressors your ways; and ungodly men shall return to you.

Deliver me from blood guiltiness, O God, the God of my salvation: then my tongue shall joyfully declare your righteousness.

O Lord, you shall open my lips; and my mouth shall declare your praise.

If you desired sacrifice, I would have given it: you will not take pleasure in whole-burnt-offerings.

Sacrifice to God is a broken spirit: a broken and humbled heart God will not despise.

Do good, O Lord, to Zion in your good pleasure; Let the walls of Jerusalem be rebuilt.

Then shall you be pleased with a sacrifice of righteousness, with offering and whole-burnt sacrifices: then shall they offer calves upon your altar.

Then we sing the Canon, without the Heirmoi.

Ode 1. Tone 8. The Irmos.

*On crossing the water as though dry land, * escaping from Egypt * and its miseries in his flight, * the Israelite raised his voice and cried aloud, * 'To our Redeemer and our God now let us sing!'*

Troparia.

Most Holy Theotokos, save us.

By many temptations I am held fast, * and seeking salvation * come for refuge in flight to you * O Mother of God's own Word and Virgin, * from my dread dangers and troubles now rescue me.

Most Holy Theotokos, save us.

The passions torment with their assaults, * despondency's burden * presses heavily on my soul, * with the calm of your Son and God, pure Maiden, * O All-immaculate Virgin, now give me peace.

Glory to the Father, the Son, and the Holy Spirit.

To God and our Saviour, you once gave birth, * pure Maiden, I beg you, * from dread troubles may I be saved, * for as I now run to you for refuge, * it is to you that I lift both my soul and mind.

Both now and ever, and to the ages of ages. Amen.

In body and soul, sick as I am, * consider me worthy, * only Mother of our true God, * of your godly providence and kindness, * for you are good and the one who gave birth to Good.

Ode 3. The Irmos.

*You constructed the heavens' high vault, O Lord, and the Church, * has you as its builder, do you establish me in your love, * you are the pinnacle * of all desires, and foundation, * mankind's only Lover, of all who believe in you.*

Troparia.

Most Holy Theotokos, save us.

As protection I set you and as the shield of my life, * you gave birth to God, Virgin Mother, guide me as a pilot now * into your anchorage, * you the support of the faithful, * source of all good things, you alone the one all-praised.

Most Holy Theotokos, save us.

I entreat you, O Virgin, dispel the strife in my soul, * pacify, I pray you, the tempest of my despondency, * for you, O Bride of God, * gave birth to him who is calm's source, * you gave birth to Christ, you alone are the one all-praised.

Glory to the Father, the Son, and the Holy Spirit.

Benefactor is he whom you bore and cause of all good, * pour out then for all the abundant wealth of his benefits, * power to do all things, * is yours who bore Christ the mighty, * powerful in strength is he, O greatly blessed by God.

Both now and ever, and to the ages of ages. Amen.

Cruel illnesses test me, and passions most damaging, * help me, I beseech you, O Virgin, aid me, all-blameless one, * for I know you to be * the inexhaustible treasure, * never failing storehouse, of healings that have no price.

Save your servants, * from every danger, O Theotokos, * for next after God * we all fly for refuge to you * as unbreachable wall and protection.

With kindness, all-praised Theotokos, * look on the dire affliction of my body * and heal the pain of my soul.

Kathisma.

Tone 2. *Thou soughtest the heights.*

Invincible rampart, fervent intercession, * the wellspring of mercy, refuge of the world, to you * we all cry insistently, * 'Sovereign Lady, Mother who bore our God, * hasten, from perils swiftly set us free, * alone you are ever swift in our defense'.

Ode 4. The Irmos.

*I have heard, Lord, the mystery * of your dispensation, I heard and was afraid, * I have meditated on your works * and exalt and glorify your Deity.*

Troparia.

Most Holy Theotokos, save us.

I entreat you, O Bride of God, * still my passions' tumult, the tempest of my faults, * still the raging turmoil in my soul; * you who brought to birth my pilot and my Lord.

Most Holy Theotokos, save us.

As I call on you to grant me * your compassion's depths, let me know your tenderness, * you who bore the Saviour of all * who now lift their voices and sing your praise.

Glory to the Father, the Son, and the Holy Spirit.

All-Immaculate Virgin, * we acknowledge you as the Mother of our God * as we offer you our hymns of thanks, * for your many gracious gifts which we enjoy.

Both now and ever, and to the ages of ages. Amen.

As our hope and assurance, * rampart of salvation which none can overthrow * we have gained you, highly honored one, * and from every trouble you deliver us.

Ode 5. The Irmos.

*Lord, enlighten us, * with your ordinances and commands, * and with your upraised arm grant unto us your peace, * for you alone, O Lord, are Lover of humanity.*

Troparia.

Most Holy Theotokos, save us.

Fill my heart, I pray, * with your gladness and unsullied joy, * Virgin most pure, the only Mother of our God, * for you who gave birth to him who is the cause of gladness.

Most Holy Theotokos, save us.

Come, deliver us * from all dangers, Theotokos most pure, * you bore eternal liberation, * the peace which passes all understanding came to birth from you.

Glory to the Father, the Son, and the Holy Spirit.

Dissipate the fog, * Bride of God, the murk of my misdeeds, * with the illumination of your radiance, * you who gave birth to the divine and pre-eternal light.

Both now and ever, and to the ages of ages. Amen.

Heal me, Pure one * heal the sickness that afflicts my soul, * making it worthy of your kindness and your care, * and by your fervent intercession grant me health, I pray.

Ode 6. The Irmos.

*I pour out * my supplication to the Lord, * and to him I shall declare my afflictions, * for, see, my soul has been filled up with evils * and now my life has been drawn very close to Hell. * Like Jonas I appeal to you, * 'O my God, bring me up from corruption!'*

Troparia.

Most Holy Theotokos, save us.

As from death * and from corruption and decay, * when to death and to decay it became captive, * he saved my nature held fast by corruption * giving himself over to the hand of death, * O Virgin, beg your Lord and Son * from the malice of foes to deliver me.

Most Holy Theotokos, save us.

I know you * to be my life's sure guardian * its protection and shield, O pure Virgin, * you who dispel the great throng of temptations, * and drive away assaults of demon hordes, * unceasingly I plead with you, * 'From the passions' corruption deliver me.'

Glory to the Father, the Son, and the Holy Spirit.

O Maiden, * complete salvation of our souls, * we have gained you as our rampart of refuge, * as our relief in afflictions and torment, * and in your light evermore we are filled with joy. * O Sovereign Lady, save us now * from the passions and dangers which plague us.

Both now and ever, and to the ages of ages. Amen.

In sickness * and with no healing in my flesh * now I lie upon my bed, yet implore you, * as you gave birth to our God and the world's Saviour, * to him who frees us from sickness and malady, * O good one, hear me, I implore, * 'From disease's corruption now raise me up.'

Save your servants, * from every danger, O Mother of God, * for next after God * we all fly for refuge to you * as unbreachable wall and protection.

Immaculate, * who through a word gave birth to the Word * beyond explanation in the last days, * make intercession, * as you have a mother's freedom to speak.

Kontakion.

Tone 2.

Protection of Christians that cannot be put to shame, * unfailing mediation with the Maker, * do not despise the voices of us sinners as we pray; * but, in your love, be quick to help us * who cry to you with faith, * 'Hasten to intercede, * make speed to entreat, * O Theotokos', * for you ever protect those who honor you.

Tone Pl. 2.

Having placed all your hope.

Sovereign and all-holy one, * do not trust me to protection * which is merely human, * but accept the pleading of your supplicant, * anguish has hold of me, * nor can I endure * the hostile demons' arrows; * no shelter can I find, * no, nor place of refuge, wretch that I am, * from every side I am assailed, * and, save you, I find none that offers solace, * Queen of all creation, * Protection of the faithful and our hope, * do not despise my entreaty, * but take action for my good.

Theotokion.

No one who has recourse to you * goes from your presence put to shame and rejected, * O Theotokos, pure Virgin, * but asking for grace * they receive gifts and benefits * most advantageous to the plea they make.

For the afflicted, transformation * and liberation for the ailing * are you, O Theotokos, Virgin: * save your City, save us all. * To all those embattled, you are peace, * you are calm to those tossed by the tempest * the one Protection of the faithful.

Ode 7. The Irmos.

*The Three Youths from Judea * who attained to the faith of the holy Trinity * in Babylon of old, * sang out as they trampled * on the furnace's raging flames, * 'Blessed are you, O God, * the God of our Fathers!'*

Troparia.

Most Holy Theotokos, save us.

With the will to accomplish * our salvation, O Saviour, you made your dwelling place * within the Virgin's womb, * revealed her as the champion * and protection for all the world. * 'Blessed are you, O God, * the God of our Fathers!'

Most Holy Theotokos, save us.

O pure Mother implore him * who desires to grant mercy, the one you brought to birth, * that they may be set free * from faults and soul's defilements, * those who cry out with faith and sing, * 'Blessed are you, O God, * the God of our Fathers!'

Glory to the Father, the Son, and the Holy Spirit.

You revealed her who bore you * as a tower of safety, as incorruption's fount, * salvation's treasury * and doorway to repentance * for all those who now cry aloud, * 'Blessed are you, O God, * the God of our Fathers!'

Both now and ever, and to the ages of ages. Amen.

As you bore Christ the Saviour * for our sake, deign to heal from all sicknesses of the soul * and weakness of the body * those who with love and longing, * O most pure, who gave birth to God, * come close to you, to draw near * to your divine protection.

Ode 8. The Irmos.

*The King of heaven, * whose praise the Angels are singing, * all the hosts of the bodiless powers * praise him and exalt him most highly to all ages.*

Troparia.

Most Holy Theotokos, save us.

Do not despise those * who beg your help, O pure Virgin, * as they raise their song up in your honor, * praising and exalting you, Maiden, to the ages.

Most Holy Theotokos, save us.

Unending rivers * of healings you pour, O Virgin, * for all those who hymn, extol and praise you, * those whose songs exalt your Birth-Giving beyond language.

Glory to the Father, the Son, and the Holy Spirit.

You cure, O Virgin, * all my soul's weakness and sickness, * and the flesh's tormenting afflictions, * so that I may sing of your glory, Highly Favored.

Both now and ever, and to the ages of ages. Amen.

The passions' onslaughts * and the assaults of temptations * you, O Virgin, repel and drive from us, * wherefore we shall praise and hymn you to all ages.

Ode 9. The Irmos.

*We who through you, O Virgin, * have been saved confess you * to be most truly the one who gave birth to God, * with all the choirs of the heavens you we now magnify.*

Troparia.

Most Holy Theotokos, save us.

Do not reject my weeping, * tears that flow unceasing, * for you, O Virgin, gave birth to our Savior Christ, * and it is he who has wiped every tear from every face.

Most Holy Theotokos, save us.

Come, fill my heart, O Virgin, * fill my heart with gladness, * for you received in his fullness the joy of all, * and made the pain and the sadness of sin now disappear.

Most Holy Theotokos, save us.

O Virgin, be the haven, * shelter and protection * of those who flee to you, rampart unshakeable, * may they have as their refuge, their gladness and their joy.

Glory to the Father, the Son, and the Holy Spirit.

Dispel the fog of error, * ignorance's darkness, * and let your light's rays, O Virgin, illumine those * who with devotion proclaim you the Theotokos.

Both now and ever, and to the ages of ages. Amen.

Heal one laid low and wretched, * in a place of sickness, * a place, O Virgin, of ill and of wretchedness, * grant transformation from weakness and feebleness to health.

And immediately:

It is truly right to call you blest, * O Theotokos, the ever blessed, * you who are most pure and the Mother of our God.

Greater in honor than the Cherubim * and beyond compare more glorious than the Seraphim, * without corruption * you gave birth to God the Word; * the true Theotokos, * we magnify you.

We sing the following Megalynaria.

Higher than the heavens is she by far, * and yet more resplendent than the sun with its blazing rays, * she who has delivered * us from the curse's power, * in hymns now let us honor * her who rules all the world.

From the swarming multitude of my sins, * both my soul and body are now weakened, they are both sick, * O Most Highly Favored, * to you I run for refuge, * the hope of those who have none, * grant me, I pray you, your help.

Mother of the One who redeemed us all, * hear the supplications your unworthy household makes, * be our intercessor * with him, the One born from you, * the world's true Sovereign Lady, * become our Advocate.

Fervently and joyfully we now sing * hymns and odes to you, the all-praised Theotokos, * with the Lord's Forerunner * and all the Saints in heaven, * implore your Son, O Mother, * to show us pity now.

Let the impious' lips be bereft of speech, * who do not worship this your icon, the all-revered, * this which was depicted * by Luke, the Lord's Apostle, * the icon with the title, * 'She who points out the Way.'

All you hosts of heaven, the Angel Ranks, * John, the Lord's Forerunner, the Apostles, the holy Twelve, * Saints beyond all number, * with our God's own Mother, * make intercession for us, * that we may all be saved.

Holy God, Holy Mighty, Holy Immortal, have mercy on us. (x3)

Glory to the Father, and the Son, and the Holy Spirit, now and forever and to the ages of ages. Amen.

All-holy Trinity, have mercy on us. Lord, forgive our sins. Master, pardon our transgressions. Holy One, visit and heal our infirmities for the glory of Your name.

Lord, have mercy. *(x3)* Glory to the Father, and the Son, and the Holy Spirit, now and forever and to the ages of ages. Amen.

Our Father, who art in heaven, hallowed be Thy name. Thy kingdom come. Thy will be done, on earth as it is in heaven. Give us this day our daily bread; and forgive us our trespasses, as we forgive those who trespass against us. And lead us not into temptation, but deliver us from the evil one.

Through the prayers of our Holy Fathers, Lord Jesus Christ our God, have mercy upon us and save us. Amen.

And the following:

Troparia of Compunction.

Tone 6.

Have mercy on us, Lord, have mercy on us; for we sinners, lacking all defense, offer you, as our Master, this supplication: have mercy on us.

Glory to the Father, the Son, and the Holy Spirit.

Lord, have mercy on us, for in you we have put our trust. Do not be very angry with us, nor remember our iniquities. But look on us now, as you are compassionate, and rescue us from our enemies. For you are our God, and we are your people; we are all the work of your hands, and we have called on your name.

Both now and ever, and to the ages of ages. Amen.

Open the gate of compassion to us, blessed Theotokos; hoping in you, may we not fail. Through you may we be delivered from adversities, for you are the salvation of the Christian race.

Troparia.

Tone 2. *When he took you down.*

All those, loving Virgin, you protect, * with your mighty hand, who in faith come * to seek refuge with you; * for we sinners, bowed beneath the weight of many faults, * have no other who in our dangers and our afflictions * is ever-present intercessor before God, * Mother of God, the Most High, * whence we fall before you, 'Deliver * all your servants in every predicament.'

Same Melody.

Joy of all who are afflicted, * champion of all dealt injustice, * the food for those who are in need, * you, the stranger's advocate, support and staff of the blind, * loving care of the sick are you, to all who are crushed down * shield, defense and aid are you, the orphan's succor and help, * Mother of our God the Most High, * hasten, All-Immaculate, hasten, * hear our prayer, deliver all your servants.

Tone Pl. 4.

Accept the pleadings * of your servants, O Lady, * and rescue us from every constraint and affliction.

Tone 2.

All my hope I lay on you, * Mother of God. * Guard me beneath your protection.

During the 15 days of August,
instead of the above, the following are sung:

Exaposteilaria.

Tone 3.

Apostles, you assembled here * brought here from the earth's furthest limits, * here in the bounds of Gethsemane * I bid you inter my body. * And you, my Son and my God, * my dear Son, receive my spirit.

O sweetness of the Angels, * the joy of all those in distress, * the Virgin Mother of the Lord, * you are the protection of Christians, * come to my aid, deliver me * from the eternal torments.

For you I have as advocate * before the God who loves mankind, * do not expose what I have done * before the sight of the Angels, * and I entreat you, O Virgin, * pray, come to my aid, come swiftly.

O Tower wreathed in gold, * O glorious Twelve-walled City, * The Throne from which the sun pours down, * the Seat of the King of all, * O wonder beyond understanding! * How is it you suckle the Master?

Through the prayers of our Holy Fathers, Lord Jesus Christ our God, have mercy upon us and save us. Amen.

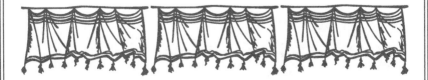

PRAYERS BEFORE MEALS

Before Breakfast

Through the prayers of our Holy Fathers, Lord Jesus Christ our God, have mercy upon us and save us. Amen.

Our Father, who art in heaven, hallowed be Thy name. Thy kingdom come. Thy will be done, on earth as it is in heaven. Give us this day our daily bread; and forgive us our trespasses, as we forgive those who trespass against us. And lead us not into temptation, but deliver us from the evil one.

Glory to the Father and to the Son and to the Holy Spirit, both now and for ever and until the ages of ages. Amen.

Lord, have mercy. *(x3)*

Through the prayers of our Holy Fathers, Lord Jesus Christ our God, have mercy upon us and save us.

Christ our God, bless the food and drink of your servants, for you are holy always, now and forever and to the ages of ages. Amen.

Thanksgiving After Breakfast

We thank you, Christ our God, for you have satisfied us with earthly gifts. Do not deprive us of your heavenly kingdom, but as you, O Saviour, came among your disciples and gave them peace, come among us also and save us. Amen.

Prayers Before Lunch

Through the prayers of the holy Fathers, Lord Jesus Christ our God, have mercy upon us. Amen.

Our Father, who art in heaven, hallowed be Thy name. Thy kingdom come. Thy will be done, on earth as it is in heaven. Give us this day our daily bread; and forgive us our trespasses, as we forgive those who trespass against us. And lead us not into temptation, but deliver us from the evil one.

Glory to the Father and to the Son and to the Holy Spirit, both now and forever and until the ages of ages. Amen.

Lord, have mercy. *(x3)*

Through the prayers of our Holy Fathers, Lord Jesus Christ our God, have mercy upon us and save us. Amen.

Christ our God, bless the food and drink of your servants, for you are holy always, now and forever and to the ages of ages. Amen.

Thanksgiving After Lunch

We thank you, Christ our God, for you have satisfied us with earthly gifts. Do not deprive us of your heavenly kingdom, but as you, O Saviour, came among your disciples and gave them peace, come among us also and save us.

Prayers Before Dinner

The poor shall eat and be satisfied, and they who seek the Lord shall praise him, their hearts shall live to the ages of ages.

Through the prayers of our Holy Fathers, Lord Jesus Christ our God, have mercy upon us and save us. Amen.

Glory to the Father and to the Son and to the Holy Spirit, both now and forever and until the ages of ages. Amen.

Lord, have mercy. *(x3)*

Christ our God, bless the food and the drink of your servants, for you are holy always, now and forever and to the ages of ages. Amen.

Thanksgiving After Dinner

Through the prayers of our Holy Fathers, Lord Jesus Christ our God, have mercy upon us and save us. Amen.

Glory to the Father and to the Son and to the Holy Spirit, both now and for ever and until the ages of ages. Amen.

Lord, have mercy. *(x3)*

Lord, you have gladdened our hearts in your creation, and we have rejoiced in the work of your hands. The light of your countenance has shined upon us, Lord. You have gladdened our hearts. We have been satisfied with the good things of the earth.

Blessed is God, who always has mercy upon us and nourishes us from his bountiful gifts by his grace and love.

We shall sleep in peace and repose in you, for you alone, Lord, have sustained us in hope, now and forever and to the ages of ages. Amen.

Behold the place where they lay Him...

THE PASCHAL HOURS

From Easter Sunday until the Saturday of renewal week, in place of morning and evening prayers, compline, and the thanksgiving prayers after communion, the following is read:

In the name of the Father, and of the Son, and of the Holy Spirit. Amen.

Christ is risen from the dead, by death trampling down upon death, and to those in the tombs bestowing life. *(x3)*

Having seen the Resurrection of Christ, let us worship the Holy Lord Jesus, the only sinless one. We worship your Cross, O Christ, and we hymn and glorify your holy Resurrection. For you are our God, we know no other but you, we name you by name. Come all the faithful, let us worship the holy Resurrection of Christ; for behold through the Cross, joy has come in all the world. Ever blessing the Lord, we hymn his Resurrection. For having endured the Cross for us, he has destroyed death by death. *(x3)*

When those who were with Mary came, anticipating the dawn, and found the stone rolled away from the sepulcher, they heard from the Angel, 'Why do you seek among the dead, as though he were mortal, the One who exists in everlasting light. See the grave clothes. Run and proclaim to the world that the Lord has been raised, and has put death to death; for he is the Son of God, who saves the human race.

Though you descended into the tomb, O Immortal, yet you destroyed the power of Hades; and you arose as victor,

O Christ God, calling to the Myrrh-bearing women: Rejoice! and giving peace to your Apostles, O you who grant resurrection to the fallen.

With your body, O Christ, you were in the tomb, with your soul in Hell as God, in Paradise with the Thief, on the throne with Father and the Spirit, filling all things, yet yourself uncircumscribed.

Glory to the Father, and to the Son, and to the Holy Spirit.

How life-giving, how much more beautiful than paradise, and truly more resplendent than any royal palace proved Thy grave, the source of our resurrection, O Christ.

Both now and for ever and to the ages of ages. Amen.

Rejoice, divine and hallowed dwelling of the Most High, for through you, Mother of God, joy has been given to those who cry, 'Blessed are you among women, spotless Lady!'

Lord have mercy *(x40)*

Glory to the Father, and to the Son, and to the Holy Spirit. Both now and for ever and to the ages of ages. Amen.

Greater in honor than the Cherubim, and beyond compare more glorious than the Seraphim, without corruption you gave birth to God the Word, truly the Mother of God we magnify you.

Through the prayers of our Holy Fathers, Lord Jesus Christ our God, have mercy upon us and save us. Amen.

If at Compline we also say the following prayer, if not, proceed with "Christ is risen"... As set forth below.

Prayer of St. Basil

Blessed are you, Master almighty, who have given light to the day by the light of the sun and made the night bright with rays of fire, who have granted us to pass through the length of the day and draw near to the beginnings of the night. Hearken to our entreaty and that of all your people, and forgive all of us our sins voluntary and involuntary and send down the multitude of your mercy and acts of compassion upon your inheritance. Wall us about with your holy Angels. Arm us with the weapons of your justice. Surround us with the rampart of your truth. Guard us with your power. Deliver us from every calamity and every assault of the adversary. Grant us that the present evening with the coming night may be perfect, holy, peaceful, sinless, without stumbling, and dreamless and likewise all the days of our life; at the prayers of the holy Mother of God and of all the Saints who have been well pleasing to you since time began. Amen.

Christ is risen from the dead, by death trampling down upon death, and to those in the tombs bestowing life. (*x3*)

Glory to the Father, and to the Son, and to the Holy Spirit. Both now and for ever and to the ages of ages. Amen.

Lord, have mercy. (*x3*)

Through the prayers of our Holy Fathers, Lord Jesus Christ our God, have mercy upon us and save us. Amen.

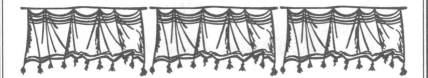

IC̅ XC̅

Ο ΩΝ

ὁ Νυμφίος τῆς Ἐκκλησίας

The Bridegroom of the Church

THE LESSER HOURS

FIRST HOUR

In the name of the Father, and of the Son, and of the Holy Spirit. Amen.

Glory to you, our God, glory to you.

Heavenly King, comforter, the Spirit of truth, who are present everywhere filling all things, Treasury of good things and Giver of life, come and dwell in us, Cleanse us of every stain, and save our souls, gracious Lord.

Holy God, Holy Mighty, Holy Immortal, have mercy on us. *(x3)*

Glory to the Father, and the Son, and the Holy Spirit, now and forever and to the ages of ages. Amen.

All-holy Trinity, have mercy on us. Lord, forgive our sins. Master, pardon our transgressions. Holy One, visit and heal our infirmities for the glory of Your name.

Lord, have mercy. *(x3)* Glory to the Father, and the Son, and the Holy Spirit, now and forever and to the ages of ages. Amen.

Our Father, who art in heaven, hallowed be Thy name. Thy kingdom come. Thy will be done, on earth as it is in heaven. Give us this day our daily bread; and forgive us our trespasses, as we forgive those who trespass against us. And lead us not into temptation, but deliver us from the evil one.

Through the prayers of our Holy Fathers, Lord Jesus Christ our God, have mercy upon us and save us. Amen.

Glory to the Father, and the Son, and the Holy Spirit, now and forever and to the ages of ages. Amen.

Come, let us worship and fall down before the King, our God.

Come, let us worship and fall down before Christ, the King, our God.

Come, let us worship and fall down before Christ himself, the King, our God.

Metanias (x3), then the Psalms.

Psalm 5

Hearken to my words, O Lord, attend to my cry. Attend to the voice of my supplication, my King and my God: for to you, O Lord, will I pray.

In the morning you shall hear my voice: in the morning I will stand beside you, and I will see

For you are not a god that desires iniquity; neither shall the worker of wickedness dwell with you.

Neither shall the transgressors continue in your sight: you hate, O Lord, all those who work iniquity.

You will destroy all that speak falsehood: the Lord abhors the bloody and deceitful man.

But I will enter into your house in the multitude of your mercy: I will worship in your fear toward your holy temple.

Lead me, O Lord, in your righteousness because of my enemies; make my way plain before your face.

For there is no truth in their mouth; their heart is vain; their throat is an open tomb; with their tongues they have used deceit.

Judge them, O God; let them fail of their counsels: cast them out according to the abundance of their ungodliness; for they have provoked you, O Lord.

But let all that trust on you be glad in you: they shall exult for ever and you shall dwell in them; and all that love your name shall rejoice in you.

For you, Lord, shall bless the righteous: you have surrounded us as with a shield of favor.

Psalm 89

Lord, you have been our refuge in all generations.

Before the mountains existed and before the earth and the world were formed, even from age to age, You exist!

Do not send a man back to his low place, whereas you said, Return, you sons of men.

For a thousand years in your sight are as the yesterday which is past and as a watch in the night.

Years shall be vanity to them: let the morning pass away as grass.

In the morning let it flower and pass away: in the evening let it droop, let it be withered and dried up.

For we have perished in your anger and in your wrath we have been troubled.

You have set our transgressions before you: our age is in the light of your countenance.

For all our days have gone and we have passed away in your wrath: our years have spun out their tale as a spider.

As for the days of our years, in them are seventy years; and if men should be in strength, eighty years: yet the greater part of them would be labor and trouble; for weakness overtakes us and we shall be chastened.

Who knows the power of your wrath?

And who knows how to number his days because of the fear of your wrath? So manifest your right hand and those who are instructed in wisdom in the heart.

Return, O Lord, how long will it be? And be entreated concerning your servants.

We have been satisfied in the morning with your mercy; we have exulted and rejoiced.

Let us rejoice in all our days, in return for the days by which you did afflict us, the years by which we saw evil.

Look upon your servants and upon your works; and guide their children.

Let the radiance of the Lord our God be upon us: and direct for us the works of our hands.

Psalm 100

I will sing to you, O Lord, of mercy and judgment;

I will sing a psalm, and I will be wise in a blameless way. When will you come to me? I walked in the innocence of my heart, in the midst of my house.

I have not set before my eyes any unlawful thing; I have hated transgressors.

A perverse heart has not cleaved to me; I have not known an evil man, since he turns away from me.

Whoever speaks secretly against his neighbor, I have driven away from me: he that is proud in look and insatiable in heart with such a person I have not eaten.

My eyes shall be upon the faithful of the land, so that they may dwell with me: he that walked in a perfect way is the one who has ministered to me.

The proud has not dwelt in the midst of my house; the unjust speaker has not prospered in my sight.

Early on did I kill all the sinners of the land, so that I might remove from the city of the Lord all that work iniquity.

Glory to the Father, and the Son, and the Holy Spirit, now and forever and to the ages of ages. Amen.

Alleluia. *(x3)* Lord, have mercy. *(x3)*

Glory to the Father and to the Son and to the Holy Spirit.

The Apolytikion of the day

Both now and forever and until the ages of ages. Amen.

Theotokion:

What shall we call you, O Full of grace? Heaven? For you made the Sun of righteousness to dawn. Paradise? For you made the flower of incorruption blossom. Virgin? For you remained incorrupt. Pure Mother? For you held in your holy embrace a Son who is the God of all. Implore him that our souls may be saved.

And immediately:

Direct my steps according to your word, and let no iniquity lord it over me.

Deliver me from the slander of men, and I shall keep your commandments.

Let your face shine on your servant, and teach me your statutes.

Let my mouth be filled with your praise, O Lord, that I may hymn your glory, all day long your splendor.

Then:

Holy God, Holy Mighty, Holy Immortal, have mercy on us. *(x3)*

Glory to the Father, and the Son, and the Holy Spirit, now and forever and to the ages of ages. Amen.

All-holy Trinity, have mercy on us. Lord, forgive our sins. Master, pardon our transgressions. Holy One, visit and heal our infirmities for the glory of Your name.

Lord, have mercy. *(x3)* Glory to the Father, and the Son, and the Holy Spirit, now and forever and to the ages of ages. Amen.

Our Father, who art in heaven, hallowed be Thy name. Thy kingdom come. Thy will be done, on earth as it is in heaven. Give us this day our daily bread; and forgive us our trespasses, as we forgive those who trespass against us. And lead us not into temptation, but deliver us from the evil one.

Through the prayers of our Holy Fathers, Lord Jesus Christ our God, have mercy upon us and save us. Amen.

The Kontakion of the Saint, if there is one, or of the current Feast, or of the day of the week. But on Sunday we say the Hypakoï of the Tone.

Lord, have mercy. *(x40)*

At every time and at every hour, in heaven and on earth worshiped and glorified, Christ God, long-suffering, great in mercy, great in compassion, loving the just and merciful to sinners, calling all to salvation by the promise of the blessings to come; do you, Lord, yourself accept our entreaties at this hour, and direct our lives to your commandments. Sanctify our souls, purify our bodies, correct our thoughts, cleanse our ideas and deliver us from every distress, evil, and pain. Wall us about with your holy Angels, that protected and guided by their host we may reach the unity of the faith and the knowledge of your unapproachable glory; for you are blessed to the ages of ages. Amen.

Lord, have mercy. *(x3)* Glory to the Father, and the Son, and the Holy Spirit, now and forever and to the ages of ages. Amen.

Greater in honor than the Cherubim, and beyond compare more glorious than the Seraphim, without corruption you gave birth to God the Word, truly the Mother of God we magnify you.

Through the prayers of our Holy Fathers, Lord Jesus Christ our God, have mercy upon us and save us. Amen.

Prayer of the First Hour

Christ, the true light, who enlighten and hallow everyone who comes into the world, may the light of your countenance be signed upon us, that in it we may see your unapproachable light; and direct our steps to the doing of your commandments; at the intercessions of your most pure Mother and of all your Saints. Amen.

To you my Champion and Commander, I your city saved from disasters dedicate, O Mother of God, hymns of victory and thanksgiving; but as you have unassailable might from every kind of danger now deliver me, that I may cry to you: Rejoice, Bride without bridegroom!

Glory to the Father, and the Son, and the Holy Spirit, now and forever and to the ages of ages. Amen.

Through the prayers of our Holy Fathers, Lord Jesus Christ our God, have mercy upon us and save us. Amen.

THIRD HOUR

In the name of the Father, and of the Son, and of the Holy Spirit. Amen.

Glory to you, our God, glory to you.

Heavenly King, comforter, the Spirit of truth, who are present everywhere filling all things, Treasury of good things and Giver of life, come and dwell in us, Cleanse us of every stain, and save our souls, gracious Lord.

Holy God, Holy Mighty, Holy Immortal, have mercy on us. (x3)

Glory to the Father, and the Son, and the Holy Spirit, now and forever and to the ages of ages. Amen.

All-holy Trinity, have mercy on us. Lord, forgive our sins. Master, pardon our transgressions. Holy One, visit and heal our infirmities for the glory of Your name.

Lord, have mercy. (x3) Glory to the Father, and the Son, and the Holy Spirit, now and forever and to the ages of ages. Amen.

Our Father, who art in heaven, hallowed be Thy name. Thy kingdom come. Thy will be done, on earth as it is in heaven. Give us this day our daily bread; and forgive us our trespasses, as we forgive those who trespass against us. And lead us not into temptation, but deliver us from the evil one.

Through the prayers of our Holy Fathers, Lord Jesus Christ our God, have mercy upon us and save us. Amen.

Lord, have mercy. *(x12)* Glory to the Father, and the Son, and the Holy Spirit, now and forever and to the ages of ages. Amen.

Come, let us worship and fall down before the King, our God.

Come, let us worship and fall down before Christ, the King, our God.

Come, let us worship and fall down before Christ himself, the King, our God.

Metanias (x3), then the Psalms.

Psalm 16

Hearken, O Lord of my righteousness, attend to my petition; give ear to my prayer not uttered with deceitful lips.

Let my judgment come forth from your presence; let my eyes behold righteousness.

You have proved my heart; you have visited me by night; you have tried me as with fire and unrighteousness has not been found in me:

That my mouth shall not speak the works of men, for the sake of the words of your lips I have kept hard ways.

Direct my steps in your paths, that my steps may not slip.

I have cried, for you heard me, O God: incline your ear to me and hearken to my words.

Show the marvels of your mercies, you that save those who hope in you.

Keep me as the apple of the eye from those who resist your right hand: you shall screen me by the covering of your wings,

From the face of the ungodly that have afflicted me: my enemies have encircled my soul.

They have enclosed themselves with their own fat: their mouth has spoken pride.

They have now cast me out and surrounded me: they have set their eyes so as to bow them down to the ground.

They laid wait for me as a lion ready for prey and like a young lion dwelling in secret places.

Arise, O Lord, prevent them and cast them down: deliver my soul from the ungodly: draw your sword from the enemies of your hand.

O Lord, destroy them from the earth; scatter them in their life, though their belly has been filled with your hidden treasures:

They have been satisfied with uncleanness, and they have left the remnant of their possessions to their young children.

But I shall appear in righteousness before your face: I shall be satisfied when your glory appears.

Psalm 24

To you, O Lord, have I lifted up my soul.

O my God, I have trusted in you: let me not be put to shame, neither let my enemies laugh me to scorn.

For none of those who wait on you shall in any way be ashamed: But let those who transgress without cause be put to shame.

Show me your ways, O Lord; and teach me your paths.

Lead me in your truth, teach me: for you are God my Savior: and I have waited on you all the day.

Remember your compassions, O Lord and your mercies, for they are from everlasting.

Do not remember the sins of my youth, nor my sins of ignorance: remember me according to your mercy, for your goodness' sake, O Lord.

Good and upright is the Lord: therefore will he instruct sinners in the way.

The meek will he guide in judgment: the meek will he teach his ways.

All the ways of the Lord are mercy and truth to those who seek his covenant and his testimonies.

For your name's sake, O Lord, be merciful to my sin; for it is great.

Who is the man that fears the Lord? The Lord shall instruct him in the way which he has chosen.

His soul shall dwell in prosperity; and his seed shall inherit the earth.

The Lord is the strength of those who fear him; and his covenant is to manifest truth to them.

My eyes are continually to the Lord; for he shall draw my feet out of the snare.

Look upon me and have mercy upon me; for I am an only child and poor.

The afflictions of my heart have been multiplied; deliver me from my distress.

Look upon my affliction and my trouble; and forgive all my sins.

Look upon my enemies; for they have been multiplied; and they have hated me with unjust hatred.

Keep my soul and deliver me: let me not be put to shame for I have hoped in you.

The innocent and upright have joined themselves to me: for I waited for you, O Lord.

Deliver Israel, O God, out of all his afflictions.

Psalm 50

Have mercy upon me, O God, according to your great mercy; according to the multitude of your compassions blot out my transgression.

Wash me thoroughly from my iniquity and cleanse me from my sin.

For I am conscious of my iniquity; and my sin is continually before me.

Against you alone have I sinned and done evil before you: that you might be justified in your sayings and overcome in your judgments.

For, behold, I was conceived in iniquities and in sins did my mother conceive me.

For, behold, you love truth: you have manifested to me the secret and hidden things of your wisdom.

You shall sprinkle me with hyssop and I shall be purified: you shall wash me and I shall be made whiter than snow.

You shall cause me to hear gladness and joy: the afflicted bones shall rejoice.

Turn away your face from my sins and blot out all my iniquities.

Create in me a clean heart, O God; and renew a right spirit in my inner being.

Do not cast me away from your presence; and do not remove your holy Spirit from me.

Restore to me the joy of your salvation: establish me with your guiding Spirit.

Then will I teach transgressors your ways; and ungodly men shall return to you.

Deliver me from blood guiltiness, O God, the God of my salvation: then my tongue shall joyfully declare your righteousness.

O Lord, you shall open my lips; and my mouth shall declare your praise.

If you desired sacrifice, I would have given it: you will not take pleasure in whole-burnt-offerings.

Sacrifice to God is a broken spirit: a broken and humbled heart God will not despise.

Do good, O Lord, to Zion in your good pleasure; Let the walls of Jerusalem be rebuilt.

Then shall you be pleased with a sacrifice of righteousness, with offering and whole-burnt sacrifices: then shall they offer calves upon your altar.

Glory to the Father, and the Son, and the Holy Spirit, now and forever and to the ages of ages. Amen.

Alleluia, Alleluia, Alleluia. Glory to you, O God. *(x3)*

Metanias (x3)

Lord, have mercy. Lord, have mercy. Lord, have mercy.

Glory to the Father and to the Son and to the holy Spirit.

Then the Apolytikion of the day. If there are two feasts the first Apolytikion is said before Glory and the second after it.

Both now and for ever, and to the ages of ages. Amen.

Theotokion.

Mother of God, you are the true vine, who gave bud to the fruit of life; we implore you, Sovereign Lady, intercede together with the Apostles and all the Saints that he have mercy on our souls.

Then at once:

Blessed is the Lord God, blessed is the Lord day by day; may the God of our salvation give us prosperity.

Then:

Holy God, Holy Mighty, Holy Immortal, have mercy on us. *(x3)*

Glory to the Father, and the Son, and the Holy Spirit, now and forever and to the ages of ages. Amen.

All-holy Trinity, have mercy on us. Lord, forgive our sins. Master, pardon our transgressions. Holy One, visit and heal our infirmities for the glory of Your name.

Lord, have mercy. *(x3)* Glory to the Father, and the Son, and the Holy Spirit, now and forever and to the ages of ages. Amen.

Our Father, who art in heaven, hallowed be Thy name. Thy kingdom come. Thy will be done, on earth as it is in heaven. Give us this day our daily bread; and forgive us our trespasses, as we forgive those who trespass against us. And lead us not into temptation, but deliver us from the evil one.

Through the prayers of our Holy Fathers, Lord Jesus Christ our God, have mercy upon us and save us. Amen.

Then the Kontakion of the day. On Sunday the Ypakoï.

Then:

Lord, have mercy. *(x40)*

At every time and at every hour, in heaven and on earth worshiped and glorified, Christ God, long-suffering, great in mercy, great in compassion, loving the just and merciful to sinners, calling all to salvation by the promise of the blessings to come; do you, Lord, yourself accept our entreaties at this hour, and direct our lives to your commandments. Sanctify our souls, purify our bodies, correct our thoughts, cleanse our ideas and deliver us from every distress, evil, and pain. Wall us about with your holy Angels, that protected and guided by their host we may reach the unity of the faith and the knowledge of your unapproachable glory; for you are blessed to the ages of ages. Amen.

Lord, have mercy. *(x3)* Glory to the Father, and the Son, and the Holy Spirit, now and forever and to the ages of ages. Amen.

Greater in honor than the Cherubim, and beyond compare more glorious than the Seraphim, without corruption you gave birth to God the Word, truly the Mother of God we magnify you.

Through the prayers of our Holy Fathers, Lord Jesus Christ our God, have mercy upon us and save us. Amen.

Prayer of St Mardarios

God and Master, Father almighty, Lord, only begotten Son, Jesus Christ and Holy Spirit, one godhead, one power, have mercy on me a sinner; and by the judgments which you know, save me your unworthy servant; for you are blessed to the ages of ages. Amen.

And at once we start the Sixth Hour.

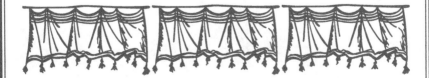

SIXTH HOUR

Come, let us worship and fall down before the King, our God.

Come, let us worship and fall down before Christ, the King, our God.

Come, let us worship and fall down before Christ himself, the King, our God.

Metanias (x3), then the Psalms.

Psalm 53

Save me, O God, by your name and judge me by your might.

O God, hear my prayer; hearken to the words of my mouth.

For strangers have risen up against me and mighty men have sought my life: they have not set God before them.

For Behold! God assists me; and the Lord is the helper of my soul.

He shall return evil to my enemies; and utterly destroy them in your truth.

I will willingly sacrifice to you: I will give thanks to your name, O Lord; for it is good.

For you have delivered me out of all affliction and my eye has seen my desire upon my enemies.

Psalm 54

Hearken, O God, to my prayer; and disregard not my supplication.

Attend to me and hearken to me: I was grieved in my meditation and troubled; because of the voice of the enemy and because of the oppression of the sinner.

For they brought iniquity against me and were filled with fierce anger against me.

My heart was troubled within me; and the fear of death fell upon me.

Fear and trembling came upon me and darkness covered me.

I said: O that I had wings as those of a dove! then would I flee away and be at rest.

Behold! I have fled afar off and dwelt in the wilderness.

I waited for him that should deliver me from distress of spirit and tempest.

Destroy, O Lord and divide their tongues: for I have seen iniquity and denial of truth in the city.

Day and night he shall go around it upon its walls: Iniquity, sorrow and unrighteousness are in the midst of it;

And usury and craft have not failed from its streets.

If an enemy had reproached me, I would have endured it; and if one who hated me had spoken boastfully against me, I would have hidden myself from him.

But you, O man like minded, my guide and my acquaintance, who in companionship with me sweetened our food: we walked in the house of God in concord.

Let death come upon them, Let them go down alive into hades, for iniquity is in their dwellings, in the midst of them.

I cried to God and the Lord listened to me.

Evening, morning and at noon I will declare and make known my wants: He shall hear my voice.

He shall deliver my soul in peace from those who draw near to me: for they were with me in many cases.

God shall hear and bring them low, even he that has existed from eternity. Because they suffer no reverse they have not feared God.

He has reached forth his hand for retribution; they have profaned his covenant.

They were scattered at the anger of his countenance and his heart drew near them. His words were smoother than oil, yet they are as darts.

Cast your care upon the Lord, He shall sustain you; he shall never suffer the righteous to be moved.

But you, O God, shall bring them down to the pit of destruction; bloody and crafty men shall not live out half their days; but I will hope in you, O Lord.

Psalm 90

He that dwells in the help of the Highest, shall sojourn under the shelter of the God of heaven.

He shall say to the Lord, You are my helper and my refuge: my God; I will hope in him.

For he shall deliver you from the snare of the hunters, from every troublesome matter.

He shall overshadow you with his shoulders and you shall trust under his wings: his truth shall cover you with a shield.

You shall not be afraid of terror by night; nor of the arrow flying by day;

Nor of the evil thing that creeps in the darkness; nor of calamity and the evil spirit at noon-day.

A thousand may fall at your side and ten thousand at your right hand; but it shall not come near you.

Only with your eyes shall you observe and see the reward of sinners.

For you, O Lord, are my hope: you have made the Most High your refuge.

No evils shall come upon you and no scourge shall draw night to your dwelling.

For he shall give his angels charge concerning you, to keep you in all your ways.

They shall bear you up on their hands, for fear that at any time you dash your foot against a stone.

You shall tread on the viper and the cobra, and you shall trample on the lion and dragon.

For he has hoped in me and I will deliver him: I will protect him, because he has known my name.

He shall call upon me and I will hearken to him: I am with him in affliction; I will deliver him and glorify him.

I will satisfy him with length of days and show him my salvation.

Glory to the Father, and the Son, and the Holy Spirit, now and forever and to the ages of ages. Amen.

Alleluia, Alleluia, Alleluia. Glory to you, O God. *(x3)*

Metanias (x3)

Lord, have mercy. *(x3)*

Glory to the Father and to the Son and to the holy Spirit.

Then the Apolytikion of the day. If there are two feasts the first Apolytikion is said before Glory and the second after it.

Both now and for ever, and to the ages of ages. Amen.

Theotokion.

Because we have no boldness on account of our many sins, entreat the One born of you, O Virgin Mother of God; for a Mother's plea has great force for the kindness of the Master. Do not despise the supplications of sinners, O all-holy, for he is merciful, and able to save, he who even accepted to suffer for us.

Then at once:

Let your mercies, O Lord, come quickly to our aid, for we are utterly poor; help us, O God our Saviour, for the glory of your name. O Lord, deliver us, and have mercy on our sins, for your name's sake.

Then:

Holy God, Holy Mighty, Holy Immortal, have mercy on us. (*x3*)

Glory to the Father, and the Son, and the Holy Spirit, now and forever and to the ages of ages. Amen.

All-holy Trinity, have mercy on us. Lord, forgive our sins. Master, pardon our transgressions. Holy One, visit and heal our infirmities for the glory of Your name.

Lord, have mercy. (*x3*) Glory to the Father, and the Son, and the Holy Spirit, now and forever and to the ages of ages. Amen.

Our Father, who art in heaven, hallowed be Thy name. Thy kingdom come. Thy will be done, on earth as it is in heaven. Give us this day our daily bread; and forgive us our trespasses, as we forgive those who trespass against us. And lead us not into temptation, but deliver us from the evil one.

Through the prayers of our Holy Fathers, Lord Jesus Christ our God, have mercy upon us and save us. Amen.

Then the Kontakion of the day. On Sunday the Ypakoï.

Lord, have mercy. (*x40*)

At every time and at every hour, in heaven and on earth worshiped and glorified, Christ God, long-suffering, great in mercy, great in compassion, loving the just and merciful to sinners, calling all to salvation by the promise of the blessings to come; do you, Lord, yourself accept our entreaties at this hour, and direct our lives to your commandments. Sanctify our souls, purify our bodies, correct our thoughts, cleanse our ideas and deliver us from every distress, evil, and pain. Wall us about with your holy Angels, that protected and guided by their host we may reach the unity of the faith and the knowledge of your unapproachable glory; for you are blessed to the ages of ages. Amen.

Lord, have mercy. *(x3)* Glory to the Father, and the Son, and the Holy Spirit, now and forever and to the ages of ages. Amen.

Greater in honor than the Cherubim, and beyond compare more glorious than the Seraphim, without corruption you gave birth to God the Word; truly the Mother of God we magnify you.

Prayer of Saint Basil The Great

O God and Lord of powers, and Maker of all creation, who through the compassion of your incomprehensible mercy sent down your only-begotten Son, our Lord and Saviour, Jesus Christ, for the salvation of our race, and through his precious Cross tore up the record of our sins, and by it triumphed over the principalities and powers of darkness; do you yourself, O Master who love mankind, accept also our supplications of thanksgiving and entreaty; and deliver us from destroying and dark transgression, and from all our foes, visible and invisible, who seek to harm us. Nail down our flesh through fear of you, and do not let our hearts incline to words or thoughts of evil, but wound our souls with longing for you; that ever gazing on you and guided by the light that comes from you, seeing you the unapproachable and everlasting light, we may give thanks to you, the Father without beginning, with your only-begotten Son and your all-holy, good and life-giving Spirit, now and for ever, and to the ages of ages. Amen.

According to the Typica of the Holy Mountain the Reader at once adds:

It is truly right to call you blest, O Theotokos, the ever blessed, you who are most pure and the Mother of our God. Greater in honor than the Cherubim and beyond compare more glorious than the Seraphim, without corruption you gave birth to God the Word; truly the Mother of God, we magnify you.

Glory to the Father, and the Son, and the Holy Spirit, now and forever and to the ages of ages. Amen.

Through the prayers of our Holy Fathers, Lord Jesus Christ our God, have mercy upon us and save us. Amen.

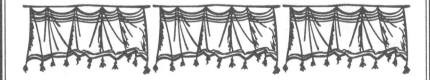

NINTH HOUR

In the name of the Father, and of the Son, and of the Holy Spirit. Amen.

Glory to you, our God, glory to you.

Heavenly King, comforter, the Spirit of truth, who are present everywhere filling all things, Treasury of good things and Giver of life, come and dwell in us, Cleanse us of every stain, and save our souls, gracious Lord.

Holy God, Holy Mighty, Holy Immortal, have mercy on us. *(x3)*

Glory to the Father, and the Son, and the Holy Spirit, now and forever and to the ages of ages. Amen.

All-holy Trinity, have mercy on us. Lord, forgive our sins. Master, pardon our transgressions. Holy One, visit and heal our infirmities for the glory of Your name.

Lord, have mercy. *(x3)* Glory to the Father, and the Son, and the Holy Spirit, now and forever and to the ages of ages. Amen.

Our Father, who art in heaven, hallowed be Thy name. Thy kingdom come. Thy will be done, on earth as it is in heaven. Give us this day our daily bread; and forgive us our trespasses, as we forgive those who trespass against us. And lead us not into temptation, but deliver us from the evil one.

Through the prayers of our Holy Fathers, Lord Jesus Christ our God, have mercy upon us and save us. Amen.

Lord, have mercy. *(x12)* Glory to the Father, and the Son, and the Holy Spirit, now and forever and to the ages of ages. Amen.

Come, let us worship and fall down before the King, our God.

Come, let us worship and fall down before Christ, the King, our God.

Come, let us worship and fall down before Christ himself, the King, our God.

Metanias (x3), then the Psalms.

Psalm 83

How lovely are your tabernacles, O Lord of Hosts! My soul longs and faints for the courts of the Lord: my heart and my flesh have exulted in the living God.

Yes, the sparrow has found herself a home and the turtle-dove a nest for herself, where she may lay her young, even your altars, O Lord of Hosts, my King and my God.

Blessed are those who dwell in your house: they will praise you unto ages of ages.

Blessed is the man whose help comes from you, O Lord; in his heart he has purposed to go up the valley of weeping,

To the place which he has appointed for there the law-giver will grant blessings. They shall go from strength to strength: the God of gods shall be seen in Zion.

O Lord God of Hosts, hear my prayer: hearken, O God of Jacob.

Behold, O God our defender and look upon the face of your anointed.

For one day in your courts is better than thousands elsewhere. I would rather have no standing in the house of God, than dwell in the tents of sinners.

For the Lord loves mercy and truth: God will give grace and glory: the Lord will not withhold good things from those who walk in innocence.

O Lord of Hosts, blessed is the man that trusts in you

Psalm 84

O Lord, you have taken pleasure in your land: you have turned back the captivity of Jacob.

You have forgiven your people their transgressions; you have covered all their sins.

You have caused all your wrath to cease: you have turned from your fierce anger.

Turn us, O God of our salvation and turn your anger away from us.

Would you be angry with us for ever? Or will you continue your wrath from generation to generation?

O God, you will turn and revive us; and your people shall rejoice in you.

Show us your mercy, O Lord and grant us your salvation.

I will hear what the Lord God will say in me: for he shall speak peace to his people, to his saints and to those who turn their heart toward him.

Moreover, his salvation is near those who fear him; that glory may dwell in our land.

Mercy and truth have met together: righteousness and peace have kissed each other.

Truth has sprung out of the earth; and righteousness has looked down from heaven.

For the Lord will give goodness; and our land shall yield her fruit.

Righteousness shall go before him; and shall set his steps in the way.

Psalm 85

O Lord, incline your ear and hearken to me; for I am poor and needy.

Preserve my soul, for I am holy; save your servant, O God, who hopes in you.

Pity me, O Lord: for to you will I cry all day long.

Rejoice the soul of your servant: for to you, O Lord, have I lifted up my soul.

For you, O Lord, are kind and gentle; plenteous in mercy to all that call upon you.

Give ear to my prayer, O Lord; and attend to the voice of my supplication.

In the day of my trouble I cried to you: for you certainly heard me.

There is none like to you, O Lord, among the gods; and there are no works comparable to your works.

All nations whom you have made shall come and worship before you, O Lord; they shall glorify your name.

For you are great and do wonders: you are the only and the great God.

Guide me, O Lord, in your way and I will walk in your truth: let my heart rejoice, that I may fear your name.

I will give you thanks, O Lord my God, with all my heart; and I will glorify your name for ever.

For your mercy is great toward me; and you have delivered my soul from the lowest hades.

O God, transgressors have risen up against me, an assembly of violent men have sought my life; they have not set you before them.

But you, O Lord God, are compassionate and merciful, long-suffering, abundant in mercy and true.

Look you upon me and have mercy on me: give your strength to your child and save the son of your handmaid.

Comfort me with a sign of your goodness; Let those who hate me see it and be ashamed; because you, O Lord, have helped me and comforted me.

And again:

Make with me a sign for good, and let those who hate me see it and be shamed; for you, Lord, have helped me and comforted me.

Glory to the Father, and the Son, and the Holy Spirit, now and forever and to the ages of ages. Amen.

Alleluia, Alleluia, Alleluia. Glory to you, O God. *(x3)* Lord, have mercy. *(x3)*

Glory to the Father and to the Son and to the holy Spirit.

Then the Apolytikion of the day. If there are two feasts, the first Apolytikion is said before Glory and the second after it.

Both now and for ever, and to the ages of ages. Amen.

Theotokion.

O Good one, born of a Virgin for our sakes and who endured crucifixion, who despoiled death by death and as God revealed resurrection, do not despise those whom you fashioned with your own hand; show your love for mankind, O Merciful; accept the Mother of God who bore you, as she intercedes for us, and save, O Saviour, a people in despair.

For your holy name's sake do not finally reject us, do not annul your covenant, do not take your mercy from us for the sake of Abraham, your beloved, and for the sake of Isaac, your servant, and Israel, your holy one.

Holy God, Holy Mighty, Holy Immortal, have mercy on us. *(x3)*

Glory to the Father, and the Son, and the Holy Spirit, now and forever and to the ages of ages. Amen.

All-holy Trinity, have mercy on us. Lord, forgive our sins. Master, pardon our transgressions. Holy One, visit and heal our infirmities for the glory of Your name.

Lord, have mercy. *(x3)* Glory to the Father, and the Son, and the Holy Spirit, now and forever and to the ages of ages. Amen.

Our Father, who art in heaven, hallowed be Thy name. Thy kingdom come. Thy will be done, on earth as it is in heaven. Give us this day our daily bread; and forgive us our trespasses, as we forgive those who trespass against us. And lead us not into temptation, but deliver us from the evil one.

Through the prayers of our Holy Fathers, Lord Jesus Christ our God, have mercy upon us and save us. Amen.

Then the Kontakion of the day. On Sunday the Ypakoï.

Lord, have mercy. *(x40)*

At every time and at every hour, in heaven and on earth worshiped and glorified, Christ God, long-suffering, great in mercy, great in compassion, loving the just and merciful to sinners, calling all to salvation by the promise of the good things to come; do you, Lord, yourself accept our entreaties at this hour, and direct our lives to your commandments. Sanctify our souls, purify our bodies, correct our thoughts, cleanse our ideas and deliver us from every distress, evil, and pain. Wall us about with your holy Angels, that protected and guided by their host we may reach the unity of the faith and the knowledge of your unapproachable glory; for you are blessed to the ages of ages. Amen.

Lord, have mercy. *(x3)* Glory to the Father, and the Son, and the Holy Spirit, now and forever and to the ages of ages. Amen.

G reater in honor than the Cherubim, and beyond compare more glorious than the Seraphim, without corruption you gave birth to God the Word, truly the Mother of God we magnify you.

Through the prayers of our Holy Fathers, Lord Jesus Christ our God, have mercy upon us and save us. Amen.

Prayer of Saint Basil the Great

M aster, Lord Jesus Christ, our God, who have long endured our transgressions, and brought us to this hour in which, hanging on the life-giving tree, you showed the good Thief the way into Paradise and destroyed death by death, have mercy also on us sinners and your unworthy servants. For we have sinned and transgressed, and are not worthy to raise our eyes and look on the height of heaven, because we have abandoned the way of your justice and walked in the will of our hearts. But we implore your unbounded goodness: spare us, O Lord, according to the multitude of your mercy, and save us for your holy name's sake, for our days have been wasted in vanity. Rescue us from the hand of our opponent, forgive us our sins, slay our carnal will, so that we, having put off the old man, may put on the new, and live for you, our Master and Benefactor; and that thus following your precepts we may reach eternal rest, where those who rejoice have their dwelling. For you are the true joy and gladness of those who love you, Christ our God, and to you we give glory, together with your Father who has no beginning, and your all-holy, good and life-giving Spirit, now and for ever, and to the ages of ages. Amen.

Glory to the Father, and the Son, and the Holy Spirit, now and forever and to the ages of ages. Amen.

Through the prayers of our Holy Fathers, Lord Jesus Christ our God, have mercy upon us and save us. Amen.

MIDNIGHT OFFICE

In the name of the Father, and of the Son, and of the Holy Spirit. Amen.

Glory to you, our God, glory to you.

Heavenly King, comforter, the Spirit of truth, who are present everywhere filling all things, Treasury of good things and Giver of life, come and dwell in us, Cleanse us of every stain, and save our souls, gracious Lord.

Holy God, Holy Mighty, Holy Immortal, have mercy on us. (x3)

Glory to the Father, and the Son, and the Holy Spirit, now and forever and to the ages of ages. Amen.

All-holy Trinity, have mercy on us. Lord, forgive our sins. Master, pardon our transgressions. Holy One, visit and heal our infirmities for the glory of Your name.

Lord, have mercy. (x3) Glory to the Father, and the Son, and the Holy Spirit, now and forever and to the ages of ages. Amen.

Our Father, who art in heaven, hallowed be Thy name. Thy kingdom come. Thy will be done, on earth as it is in heaven. Give us this day our daily bread; and forgive us our trespasses, as we forgive those who trespass against us. And lead us not into temptation, but deliver us from the evil one.

Through the prayers of our Holy Fathers, Lord Jesus Christ our God, have mercy upon us and save us. Amen.

Lord, have mercy. *(x12)* Glory to the Father, and the Son, and the Holy Spirit, now and forever and to the ages of ages. Amen.

Then the following Hymns to the Trinity. Tone 1.

On rising from sleep, we fall down before you, O Good One, and we cry to you with the Angels' hymn, O Mighty One: Holy, Holy, Holy are you, O God: through the Mother of God have mercy on us.

Glory to the Father and to the Son and to the Holy Spirit.

Tone 2.

You have roused me, Lord, from my bed and from sleep, enlighten my mind and open my heart and my lips, to sing your praise, O Holy Trinity: Holy, Holy, Holy are you, O God: through the Mother of God have mercy on us.

Both now and for ever, and to the ages of ages. Amen.

Tone 3.

The Judge will come suddenly, and the deeds of each will be laid bare; but with fear let us cry to you in the middle of the night: Holy, Holy, Holy are you, O God: through the Mother of God have mercy on us.

Lord, have mercy. *(x12)*

...and these prayers.

Prayer of Thanksgiving with Intercession

Having risen from sleep I thank you, O Holy Trinity; because through your great goodness and patience you have not been angry with me, an idler and a sinner, nor have you destroyed me in my iniquities, but you have shown your customary love for mankind and roused me, as I lay in despair, to rise before dawn and to glorify your might. And now, enlighten the eyes of my mind and open my mouth to meditate on your words, to understand your commandments and to do your will, and to sing to you with confession of heart and to hymn your all-holy name, of Father, Son and Holy Spirit, now and for ever, and to the ages of ages. Amen.

Another Prayer

Glory to you, O King, almighty God, because in your divine providence and love for mankind, you have permitted me, sinner and unworthy, to rise from sleep and to gain entrance to your holy house. Accept, too, Lord, the voice of my supplication, as you do that of your holy and spiritual Powers; and be well pleased for praise to be offered you with a pure heart and a spirit of humility from my sordid lips, that I too may become a companion of the wise virgins with the shining lamp of my soul and may glorify you, God the Word, glorified with the Father and the Spirit. Amen.

Through the prayers of our holy Fathers, Lord Jesus Christ, our God, have mercy on us.

Glory to you, our God, glory to you.

Heavenly King, comforter, the Spirit of truth, who are present everywhere filling all things, Treasury of good things and Giver of life, come and dwell in us, Cleanse us of every stain, and save our souls, gracious Lord.

Holy God, Holy Mighty, Holy Immortal, have mercy on us. *(x3)*

Glory to the Father, and the Son, and the Holy Spirit, now and forever and to the ages of ages. Amen.

All-holy Trinity, have mercy on us. Lord, forgive our sins. Master, pardon our transgressions. Holy One, visit and heal our infirmities for the glory of Your name.

Lord, have mercy. *(x3)* Glory to the Father, and the Son, and the Holy Spirit, now and forever and to the ages of ages. Amen.

Our Father, who art in heaven, hallowed be Thy name. Thy kingdom come. Thy will be done, on earth as it is in heaven. Give us this day our daily bread; and forgive us our trespasses, as we forgive those who trespass against us. And lead us not into temptation, but deliver us from the evil one.

Through the prayers of our Holy Fathers, Lord Jesus Christ our God, have mercy upon us and save us. Amen.

Come, let us worship and fall down before the King, our God.

Come, let us worship and fall down before Christ the King, our God.

Come, let us worship and fall down before Christ himself, the King, our God.

Metanias (x3), and at once

Psalm 50

Have mercy upon me, O God, according to your great mercy; according to the multitude of your compassions blot out my transgression.

Wash me thoroughly from my iniquity and cleanse me from my sin.

For I am conscious of my iniquity; and my sin is continually before me.

Against you alone have I sinned and done evil before you: that you might be justified in your sayings and overcome in your judgments.

For, behold, I was conceived in iniquities and in sins did my mother conceive me.

For, behold, you love truth: you have manifested to me the secret and hidden things of your wisdom.

You shall sprinkle me with hyssop and I shall be purified: you shall wash me and I shall be made whiter than snow.

You shall cause me to hear gladness and joy: the afflicted bones shall rejoice.

Turn away your face from my sins and blot out all my iniquities.

Create in me a clean heart, O God; and renew a right spirit in my inner being.

Do not cast me away from your presence; and do not remove your holy Spirit from me.

Restore to me the joy of your salvation: establish me with your guiding Spirit.

Then will I teach transgressors your ways; and ungodly men shall return to you.

Deliver me from blood guiltiness, O God, the God of my salvation: then my tongue shall joyfully declare your righteousness.

O Lord, you shall open my lips; and my mouth shall declare your praise.

If you desired sacrifice, I would have given it: you will not take pleasure in whole-burnt-offerings.

Sacrifice to God is a broken spirit: a broken and humbled heart God will not despise.

Do good, O Lord, to Zion in your good pleasure; Let the walls of Jerusalem be rebuilt.

Then shall you be pleased with a sacrifice of righteousness, with offering and whole-burnt sacrifices: then shall they offer calves upon your altar.

Then on weekdays we say Kathisma 17 (Psalm 118), but on Saturday we say Kathisma 9 (Psalm 64-69), See pg. 163.

Psalm 118

First Stasis

Blessed are the blameless in the way, who walk in the law of the Lord.

Blessed are those who search out his testimonies: they will diligently seek him with the whole heart.

For those who work iniquity have not walked in his ways.

You have commanded us diligently to keep your precepts.

O that my ways were directed to keep your ordinances.

Then shall I not be ashamed when I have respect to all your commandments.

I will give you thanks with uprightness of heart when I have learnt the judgments of your righteousness.

I will keep your ordinances: O forsake me not greatly.

By which shall a young man direct his way? By keeping your words.

With my whole heart have I diligently sought you: cast me not away from your commandments.

I have hidden your oracles in my heart, that I might not sin against you.

Blessed are you, O Lord: teach me your ordinances.

With my lips have I declared all the judgments of your mouth.

I have delighted in the way of your testimonies, as much as in all riches.

I will meditate on your commandments and consider your ways.

I will meditate on your ordinances: I will not forget your words.

Render a recompense to your servant: so shall I live and keep your words.

Unveil my eyes and I shall perceive the wondrous things of your law.

I am a stranger in the earth: hide not your commandments from me.

My soul has longed exceedingly for your judgments at all times.

You have rebuked the proud: cursed are those who turn aside from your commandments.

Remove from me reproach and contempt; for I have sought out your testimonies.

For princes sat and spoke against me, but your servant was meditating on your ordinances.

For your testimonies are my meditation and your ordinances are my counselors.

My soul has cleaved to the ground; revive me according to your word.

I declared my ways and you did hear me: teach me your ordinances.

Instruct me in the way of your ordinances; and I will meditate on your wondrous works.

My soul has slumbered for weariness; strengthen me with your words.

Remove from me the way of iniquity; and be merciful to me by your law.

I have chosen the way of truth; and have not forgotten your judgments.

I have cleaved to your testimonies, O Lord; do not put me to shame.

I ran the way of your commandments when you did enlarge my heart. Teach me, O Lord, the way of your ordinances and I will seek it out continually.

Instruct me and I will search out your law and keep it with my whole heart.

Guide me in the path of your commandments; for I have delighted in it.

Incline my heart to your testimonies and not to covetousness.

Turn away my eyes that I may not behold vanity: revive me in your way.

Confirm your oracle to your servant, so that he may fear you.

Take away my reproach which I have feared: for your judgments are good.

Behold, I have desired your commandments: revive me in your righteousness.

Let your mercy come upon me, O Lord; even your salvation, according to your word.

And so I shall render an answer to those who reproach me: for I have trusted in your words.

And take not the word of truth utterly out of my mouth; for I have hoped in your judgments. So shall I keep your law continually, unto ages of ages.

I walked also at large: for I sought out your commandments.

I spoke of your testimonies before kings and was not ashamed.

I meditated on your commandments, which I loved exceedingly.

I lifted up my hands to your commandments which I loved; and I meditated in your ordinances.

Remember your words to your servant, by which you have made me hope.

This has comforted me in my affliction: for your oracle has revived me.

The proud have transgressed exceedingly; but I swerved not from your law.

I remembered your judgments of old, O Lord; and I was comforted.

Despair took hold upon me, because of the sinners who forsake your law.

Your ordinances were my songs in the place of my sojourning.

I remembered your name, O Lord, in the night and kept your law.

This I had, because I diligently sought your ordinances.

You are my portion, O Lord: I said that I would keep your law.

I besought your favor with my whole heart: have mercy upon me according to your word.

I thought on your ways and turned my feet to your testimonies.

I prepared myself, and was not terrified, to keep your commandments.

The snares of sinners entangled me: but I forgot not your law.

At midnight I arose, to give thanks to you for the judgments of your righteousness.

I am a companion of all those who fear you and of those who keep your commandments.

O Lord, the earth is full of your mercy: teach me your ordinances.

You have accomplished kindly with your servant, O Lord, according to your word.

Teach me kindness and instruction and knowledge: for I have believed your commandments.

Before I was afflicted, I transgressed; therefore have I kept your word.

Good are you, O Lord; therefore in your goodness teach me your ordinances.

The injustice of the proud has been multiplied against me: but I will search out your commandments with all my heart.

Their heart has been curdled like milk; but I have meditated on your law.

It is good for me that you have afflicted me; that I might learn your ordinances.

The law of your mouth is better to me than thousands of gold and silver.

Glory to the Father, and the Son, and the Holy Spirit, now and forever and to the ages of ages. Amen.

Alleluia, Alleluia, Alleluia. Glory to you, O God. *(x3)* Lord, have mercy. *(x3)*

Glory to the Father, and the Son, and the Holy Spirit, now and forever and to the ages of ages. Amen.

Second Stasis

Your hands have made me and fashioned me: instruct me, that I may learn your commandments.

Those who fear you will see me and rejoice: for I have hoped in your words.

I know, O Lord, that your judgments are righteousness and that you in truthfulness have afflicted me.

Let, I pray you, your mercy be to comfort me, according to your word to your servant.

Let your compassions come to me, that I may live: for your law is my meditation.

Let the proud be ashamed; for they transgressed against me unjustly: but I will meditate in your commandments.

Let those who fear you and those who know your testimonies, turn to me.

Let my heart be blameless in your ordinances, that I may not be ashamed.

My soul faints for your salvation: I have hoped in your words.

My eyes failed in waiting for your word, saying when will you comfort me?

For I have become as a bottle in the frost: yet I have not forgotten your ordinances.

How many are the days of your servant? When will you execute judgment for me on those who persecute me?

Transgressors told me subtleties; but not according to your law, O Lord.

All your commandments are truth; they persecuted me unjustly; help me.

They nearly made an end of me in the earth; but I forsook not your commandments.

Revive me according to your mercy; so shall I keep the testimonies of your mouth.

Your word, O Lord, abides in heaven for ever.

Your truth endures to all generations; you have founded the earth and it abides.

The day continues by your arrangement; for all things are your servants.

Were it not that your law is my meditation, then I should have perished in my affliction.

I will never forget your ordinances; for with them you have revived me.

I am yours, save me; for I have sought out your ordinances.

Sinners laid wait for me to destroy me; but I understood your testimonies.

Have seen an end of all perfection; but your commandment is very broad.

How I loved your law, O Lord! It is my meditation all the day.

You have made me wiser than my enemies in your commandment; for it is mine for ever.

I have more understanding than all my teachers; for your testimonies are my meditation.

I understand more that the aged; because I have sought out your commandments.

I have kept back my feet from every evil way, that I might keep your words.

I have not declined from your judgments; for you have instructed me.

How sweet are your oracles to my throat! More so than honey to my mouth!

I gain understanding by your commandments: therefore I have hated every way of unrighteousness;

Your law is a lamp to my feet and a light to my paths.

I have sworn and determined to keep the judgments of your righteousness.

I have been very greatly afflicted, O Lord: revive me, according to your word.

Accept, I pray you, O Lord, the free will-offerings of my mouth and teach me your judgments.

My soul is continually in your hands; and I have not forgotten your law.

Sinners spread a snare for me; but I erred not from your commandments.

I have inherited your testimonies for ever; for they are the joy of my heart.

I have inclined my heart to perform your ordinances for ever, in return for your mercies.

I have hated transgressors; but I loved your law.

You are my helper and my supporter; I have hoped in your words.

Depart from me, you evil-doers; for I will search out the commandments of my God.

Uphold me according to your word and revive me; and make me not ashamed of my expectation.

Help me and I shall be saved; and I will meditate in your ordinances continually.

You have brought to nought all that depart from your ordinances; for their inward thought is unrighteous.

I have reckoned all the sinners of the earth as transgressors; therefore have I loved your testimonies.

Penetrate my flesh with your fear; for I am afraid of your judgments.

I have done judgment and justice; deliver me not up to those who injure me.

Receive your servant for good: let not the proud accuse me falsely.

My eyes have failed for your salvation and for the word of your righteousness.

Deal with your servant according to your mercy and teach me your ordinances.

I am your servant; instruct me and I shall know your testimonies.

It is time for the Lord to work: they have utterly broken your law.

Therefore have I loved your commandments more than gold, or the topaz.

Therefore I directed myself according to all your commandments: I have hated every unjust way.

Your testimonies are wonderful: therefore my soul has sought them out.

The manifestation of your words will enlighten and instruct the simple.

I opened my mouth and drew breath: for I earnestly longed after your commandments.

Glory to the Father, and the Son, and the Holy Spirit, now and forever and to the ages of ages. Amen.

Alleluia, Alleluia, Alleluia. Glory to you, O God. *(x3)* Lord, have mercy. *(x3)*

Glory to the Father, and the Son, and the Holy Spirit, now and forever and to the ages of ages. Amen.

Third Stasis

Look upon me and have mercy upon me, after the manner of those who love your name.

Order my steps according to your word: Let not any iniquity have dominion over me.

Deliver me from the false accusation of men: so will I keep your commandments.

Cause your face to shine upon your servant: and teach me your ordinances.

My eyes have been bathed in streams of water, because I have not kept your law.

Righteous are you, O Lord and upright are your judgments.

You have commanded righteousness and perfect truth, as your testimonies.

Your zeal has quite wasted me: because my enemies have forgotten your words.

Your word has been very fully tried; and your servant loves it.

I am young and despised: yet I have not forgotten your ordinances.

Your righteousness is an everlasting righteousness and your law is truth.

Afflictions and distresses found me: but your commandments were my meditation.

Your testimonies are an everlasting righteousness: instruct me and I shall live.

I cried with my whole heart; hear me, O Lord: I will search out your ordinances.

I cried to you; save me and I will keep your testimonies.

I arose before the dawn and cried: I hoped in your words.

My eyes prevented the dawn, that I might meditate on your oracles.

Hear my voice, O Lord, according to your mercy; revive me according to your judgment.

They have drawn near who persecuted me unlawfully; and they are far removed from your law.

You are near, O Lord; and all your ways are truth.

I have known of old concerning your testimonies, that you have founded them for ever.

Look upon my affliction and rescue me; for I have not forgotten your law.

Plead my cause and ransom me: revive me because of your word.

Salvation is far from sinners: for they have not searched out your ordinances.

Your mercies, O Lord, are many: revive me according to your judgment.

Many are those who persecute me and oppress me: but I have not declined from your testimonies.

I beheld men acting foolishly and I pined away; for they kept not your oracles.

Behold, I loved your commandments, O Lord: revive me in your mercy.

The beginning of your words is truth; and all the judgments of your righteousness endure for ever.

Princes persecuted me without a cause, but my heart feared because of your words.

I will exult because of your oracles, as one that finds much spoil.

I hate and abhor unrighteousness; but I love your law.

Seven times in a day have I praised you because of the judgments of your righteousness.

Great peace have those who love your law: and there is no stumbling-block to them.

I waited for your salvation, O Lord and loved your commandments.

My soul has kept your testimonies and loved them exceedingly.

I have kept your commandments and your testimonies; for all my ways are before you, O Lord.

Let my supplication come near before you, O Lord; instruct me according to your oracle.

Let my petition come in before you, O Lord; deliver me according to your oracle.

Let my lips utter a hymn when you shall have taught me your ordinances.

Let my tongue utter your oracles; for all your commandments are righteous.

Let your hand be prompt to save me; for I have chosen your commandments.

I have longed after your salvation, O Lord; and your law is my meditation.

My soul shall live and shall praise you; and your judgments shall help me.

I have gone astray like a lost sheep; seek your servant; for I have not forgotten your commandments.

Glory to the Father, and the Son, and the Holy Spirit, now and forever and to the ages of ages. Amen.

THE SYMBOL OF FAITH

I believe in one God, Father Almighty, Creator of heaven and earth and of all things visible and invisible.

And in one Lord Jesus Christ, the only-begotten Son of God, begotten of the Father before all ages. Light of Light, true

God of true God, begotten not created, of one essence with the Father through Whom all things were made.

Who for us men and for our salvation came down from heaven and was incarnate of the Holy Spirit and the Virgin Mary and became man.

He was crucified for us under Pontius Pilate. He suffered and was buried.

And He rose on the third day, according to the Scriptures.

He ascended into heaven and is seated at the right hand of the Father.

And He will come again with glory to judge the living and dead. His kingdom shall have no end.

And in the Holy Spirit, the Lord, the Creator of life, Who proceeds from the Father, Who together with the Father and the Son is worshiped and glorified, Who spoke through the prophets.

In one, holy, catholic, and apostolic Church.

I confess one baptism for the forgiveness of sins.

I look for the resurrection of the dead and the life of the age to come. Amen.

Holy God, Holy Mighty, Holy Immortal, have mercy on us. (x3)

Glory to the Father, and the Son, and the Holy Spirit, now and forever and to the ages of ages. Amen.

All-holy Trinity, have mercy on us. Lord, forgive our sins. Master, pardon our transgressions. Holy One, visit and heal our infirmities for the glory of Your name.

Lord, have mercy. *(x3)* Glory to the Father, and the Son, and the Holy Spirit, now and forever and to the ages of ages. Amen.

Our Father, who art in heaven, hallowed be Thy name. Thy kingdom come. Thy will be done, on earth as it is in heaven. Give us this day our daily bread; and forgive us our trespasses, as we forgive those who trespass against us. And lead us not into temptation, but deliver us from the evil one.

Through the prayers of our Holy Fathers, Lord Jesus Christ our God, have mercy upon us and save us. Amen.

Then these Troparia in Tone 8.

Behold the bridegroom is coming in the middle of the night; and blessed is the servant whom he finds watching; but unworthy is the one whom he finds idle. Take care then, my soul, not to be overcome with sleep, lest you be given up to death and shut outside the kingdom; but stay wakeful and cry, 'Holy, Holy, Holy are you, O God. Through the Mother of God have mercy on us'.

Glory to the Father and the Son and the Holy Spirit.

Consider that dread day my soul and keep watch, lighting your lamp, and bright with oil; for you do not know when the voice will come to you which says, 'Behold the Bridegroom'. Take care then, my soul, lest you doze and stay outside knocking like the five virgins; but persevere unsleeping, that you may meet Christ God with rich oil and that he may give you the divine bridal chamber of his glory.

Both now and forever and to the ages of ages. Amen.

Theotokion.

We beg you, Virgin Mother of God, unassailable wall and fortress of salvation; scatter the counsels of the foe; turn your people's grief to joy; restore your world; strengthen the devout; intercede for the peace of the world; for you, Mother of God, are our hope.

On the forefeasts, afterfeasts and Leave-taking of the feasts of the Lord and the Mother of God, instead of the above Troparia, their Apolytikion is read.

Lord, have mercy. *(x40)*

At every time and at every hour, in heaven and on earth worshiped and glorified, Christ God, long-suffering, great in mercy, great in compassion, loving the just and merciful to sinners, calling all to salvation by the promise of the good things to come; do you, Lord, yourself accept our entreaties at this hour, and direct our lives to your commandments. Sanctify our souls, purify our bodies, correct our thoughts, cleanse our ideas and deliver us from every distress, evil, and pain. Wall us about with your holy Angels, that protected and guided by their host we may reach the unity of the faith and the knowledge of your unapproachable glory; for you are blessed to the ages of ages. Amen.

Lord, have mercy. *(x3)*. Glory to the Father, and the Son, and the Holy Spirit, now and forever and to the ages of ages. Amen.

Greater in honor than the Cherubim, and beyond compare more glorious than the Seraphim, without corruption you gave birth to God the Word, truly the Mother of God we magnify you.

Through the prayers of our Holy Fathers, Lord Jesus Christ our God, have mercy upon us and save us. Amen.

In the holy and great Lent we make the three great metanias, saying to ourselves at each a line of the Prayer of St Ephrem:

Lord and Master of my life, do not give me a spirit of sloth, idle curiosity, love of power and useless chatter. *(Prostration)*

Rather accord to me, your servant, a spirit of sobriety, humility, patience and love. *(Prostration)*

Yes, Lord and King, grant me to see my own faults and not to condemn my brother; for you are blessed to the ages of ages. Amen. *(Prostration)*

Then the 12 small metanias and again a great metania and the last line of the Prayer.

Holy God, Holy Mighty, Holy Immortal, have mercy on us. *(x3)*

Glory to the Father, and the Son, and the Holy Spirit, now and forever and to the ages of ages. Amen.

All-holy Trinity, have mercy on us. Lord, forgive our sins. Master, pardon our transgressions. Holy One, visit and heal our infirmities for the glory of Your name.

Lord, have mercy. *(x3)* Glory to the Father, and the Son, and the Holy Spirit, now and forever and to the ages of ages. Amen.

Our Father, who art in heaven, hallowed be Thy name. Thy kingdom come. Thy will be done, on earth as it is in heav-

en. Give us this day our daily bread; and forgive us our trespasses, as we forgive those who trespass against us. And lead us
not into temptation, but deliver us from the evil one.

Through the prayers of our Holy Fathers, Lord Jesus Christ
our God, have mercy upon us and save us. Amen.

Lord, have mercy. *(x12)*

Then this…

Prayer of Saint Mardarios

God and Master, Father almighty, Lord, only begotten Son,
Jesus Christ, and Holy Spirit, one godhead, one power,
have mercy on me a sinner; and by the judgments which you
know, save me your unworthy servant; for you are blessed to
the ages of ages. Amen.

Note that the following prayer is said from September 22nd until Palm Sunday.

Prayer of Saint Basil the Great

Lord almighty, God of Powers and of all flesh, who dwell on
high and look on lowly things, who test hearts and minds
and know all the secrets of mortals, light without beginning
and without end, with whom there is no change nor shadow
of alteration; receive, immortal King, the supplications which
we, confident of the multitude of your mercies, offer to you
from filthy lips at the present hour of the night, and forgive us
the offenses by which we have offended in deed and word and
thought, in knowledge or in ignorance, and cleanse us from
every defilement of flesh and spirit, making us temples of your
Holy Spirit. And grant that we may pass through the whole
night of this present life with an unsleeping heart and a watchful mind, as we wait for the coming of the bright and manifest

day of your only-begotten Son, our Lord and God and Saviour, Jesus Christ, when he will come to earth with glory to
render to each according to their deeds. So that we may not
be found lifeless and slumbering, but watchful and awake in
the doing of your commandments, and that, prepared, we may
enter together the joy and the divine bridal chamber of his glory, where the sound of those who feast is unceasing and the
delight of those who see the ineffable beauty of your face is
inexpressible. For you are the true light, which enlightens and
sanctifies all things, and all creation hymns you to the ages of
ages.

*On Saturdays, instead of this prayer,
we read the prayer of St. Efstratios, See p. 173*

Prayer of Saint Basil the Great

We bless you, God most high and Lord of mercy, who
ever do with us great and unfathomable things, things
glorious and extraordinary without number, who grant us
sleep for the refreshment of our weakness and the relaxation
of the toils of our much wearied flesh. We thank you because
you have not destroyed us in our lawlessness, but have shown
us your customary love for mankind and roused us as we lay in
despair, to glorify your might. And so we implore your incom-
parable loving-kindness, enlighten the eyes of our understanding and raise our minds from the heavy sleep of idleness. Open
our mouths and fill them with your praise, that we may be able
to sing and chant and give thanks to you continually, God glorified in all and by all, the Father without beginning, with your
only begotten Son and your all-holy, good and life-giving Spirit, now and for ever, and to the ages of ages. Amen.

Then...

Come, let us worship and fall down before the King, our God.

Come, let us worship and fall down before Christ the King, our God.

Come, let us worship and fall down before Christ himself, the King, our God.

Metanias (x3) and the Psalms

Psalm 120

I lifted up my eyes to the mountains, from where my help shall come.

My help shall come from the Lord, who made the heaven and the earth.

Let not your foot be moved; Let not your keeper slumber.

Behold, he that keeps Israel shall not slumber nor sleep.

The Lord shall keep you: the Lord is your shelter upon your right hand.

The sun shall not burn you by day, neither the moon by night.

May the Lord preserve you from all evil: the Lord shall keep your soul.

The Lord shall keep your coming in and your going out, from henceforth and even forevermore.

Psalm 133

Behold now, bless you the Lord, all the servants of the Lord, who stand in the house of the Lord, in the courts of the house of our God.

Lift up your hands by night in the sanctuaries and bless the Lord.

May the Lord, who made heaven and earth, bless you out of Zion.

Glory to the Father, and the Son, and the Holy Spirit, now and forever and to the ages of ages. Amen.

Holy God, Holy Mighty, Holy Immortal, have mercy on us. *(x3)*

Glory to the Father, and the Son, and the Holy Spirit, now and forever and to the ages of ages. Amen.

All-holy Trinity, have mercy on us. Lord, forgive our sins. Master, pardon our transgressions. Holy One, visit and heal our infirmities for the glory of Your name.

Lord, have mercy. *(x3)* Glory to the Father, and the Son, and the Holy Spirit, now and forever and to the ages of ages. Amen.

Our Father, who art in heaven, hallowed be Thy name. Thy kingdom come. Thy will be done, on earth as it is in heaven. Give us this day our daily bread; and forgive us our trespasses, as we forgive those who trespass against us. And lead us not into temptation, but deliver us from the evil one.

Through the prayers of our Holy Fathers, Lord Jesus Christ our God, have mercy upon us and save us. Amen.

And the following Troparia. Tone 8.

As you are good, Lord, remember your servants and pardon them whatever sins they committed in life; for no one is sinless but you, who are able to give rest also to those who have passed over.

You who with wisdom dispose all things with love for mankind and impart to all, only Creator, that which is profitable, give rest, Lord, to the souls of your servants, for they placed their hope in you, our maker and fashioner and God.

Glory to the Father and the Son and the Holy Spirit.

With the Saints, O Christ, give rest to the souls of your servants, where there is neither toil, nor grief, nor sighing, but life without end.

Both now and forever and to the ages of ages. Amen.

All generations call you blessed, Virgin Mother of God, for in you the uncontainable, Christ our God, was well pleased to be contained. Blessed are we also with you as protection, for day and night you intercede for us and the scepters of the kingdom are strengthened by your entreaties; therefore with hymns we cry to you: Hail, full of grace. The Lord is with you.

Here during feasts of the Lord and the Mother of God their Kontakion is read.

Lord, have mercy. *(x12) And this prayer...*

Remember, Lord, our fathers and brethren who have fallen asleep in hope of resurrection to eternal life and all those who have died in piety and faith; and pardon them every offence, willing and unwilling, in word, or deed, or thought, by which they have offended. Settle them in places of light, places of green pasture, places of rest, from which all sorrow, grief and sighing have fled; where the presence of your face gives joy to all your saints from every age. Grant them and us your Kingdom and participation in your ineffable and eternal good things, and the enjoyment of your infinite and blessed life. For you are the life, the resurrection and the repose of your servants who have fallen asleep, Christ our God, and to you we give glory, together with your Father who has no beginning, and your all-holy, good and life giving Spirit, now and for ever, and to the ages of ages. Amen.

Most glorious, ever-virgin, blessed Mother of God, offer our prayer to your Son and our God, and ask that through you he may save our souls.

Prayer of Saint Ioannikios

The Father is my hope, the Son my refuge, the Holy Spirit my protection. Holy Trinity, glory to you.

All my hope I place in you, Mother of God, guard me under your protection.

And the following Troparia. Tone 6

Have mercy on us, Lord, have mercy on us; for we sinners, lacking all defense, offer you, as our Master, this supplication: have mercy on us.

Glory to the Father, and to the Son, and to the Holy Spirit.

Lord, have mercy on us, for in you we have put our trust. Do not be very angry with us, nor remember our iniquities.

But look on us now, as you are compassionate, and rescue us from our enemies. For you are our God, and we are your people; we are all the work of your hands, and we have called on your name.

Both now and for ever, and to the ages of ages. Amen.

Open the gate of compassion to us, blessed Mother of God; hoping in you, may we not fail. Through you may we be delivered from adversities, for you are the salvation of the Christian race.

Glory to the Father, and the Son, and the Holy Spirit, now and forever and to the ages of ages. Amen.

Lord, have mercy. *(x3)*

Through the prayers of our Holy Fathers, Lord Jesus Christ our God, have mercy upon us and save us. Amen.

ADDENDUM TO THE MIDNIGHT OFFICE

On Saturdays, instead of Psalm 118, we say Kathisma 9:

Psalm 64

Praise is fitting for you, O God, in Zion; and to you shall the vow be performed.

Hear my prayer; to you all flesh shall come.

The words of transgressors have overpowered us; but you pardon our sins.

Blessed is he whom you have chosen and adopted; he shall dwell in your courts; we shall be filled with the good things of your house; your temple is holy.

You are wonderful in righteousness.

Hearken to us, O God our Savior;

Your are the hope of all the ends of the earth and of those who are on the sea afar off:

You establish the mountains in your strength, being girded about with power;

You trouble the depth of the sea, and the sounds of its waves.

The nations shall be troubled and those who inhabit the ends of the earth shall be afraid of your signs; you will cause the outgoings of morning and evening to rejoice.

You have visited the earth and filled it; you have abundantly enriched it. The river of God is filled with water; you have prepared their food, for thus is how they are fed.

Satiate her furrows, multiply her fruits; the crop springing up shall rejoice in its drops.

You will bless the crown of the year because of your goodness; and your plains shall be filled with abundance.

The mountains of the wilderness shall be enriched; and the hills shall gird themselves with joy.

The rams of the flock are clothed with wool and the valleys shall abound in corn; they shall cry aloud, yes they shall sing hymns.

Psalm 65

Shout to God, all the earth.

O sing praises to his name; give glory to his praise.

Say to God, How awesome are your works! Through the greatness of your power your enemies shall lie before you.

Let all the earth worship you and sing to you; let them sing to your name.

Come and behold the works of God; he is awesome in his counsels beyond the children of men.

Who turns the sea into dry land; they shall go through the river on foot; there shall we rejoice in him,

Who by his power is Lord over the age, his eyes look upon the nations; let not those who provoke him be exalted in themselves.

Bless our God, you Gentiles and make the voice of his praise to be heard;

He revives my soul in life and does not suffer my feet to be moved.

For you, O God, have tested us; you have tried us with fire as silver is tried.

You brought us into the snare; you laid afflictions on our back.

You let men ride upon our heads; we went through the fire and water; but you brought us out into a place of refreshment.

I will go into your house with whole-burnt-offerings; I will pay you my vows,

Which my lips framed and my mouth uttered in my affliction.

I will offer to you whole-burnt-sacrifices full of marrow, with incense and rams; I will sacrifice to you oxen with goats.

Come, hear and I will share with all you who fear God, how great things he has done for my soul.

I cried to him with my mouth and exalted him with my tongue.

If I have considered iniquity in my heart, let not the Lord hearken to me.

Therefore God has listened to me; he has attended to the voice of my prayer.

Blessed be God, who has not turned away my prayer, nor removed his mercy from me.

Psalm 66

May God be merciful to us and bless us; and cause his face to shine upon us.

That men may know your way on the earth, your salvation among all nations.

Let the nations, O God, give thanks to you; let all the nations give thanks to you.

Let the nations rejoice and exult, for you shall judge the peoples in equity and shall guide the nations on the earth.

Let the peoples, O God, give thanks to you; let all the peoples give thanks to you.

The earth has yielded her fruit; let God, our God bless us.

Let God bless us; Let all the ends of the earth fear him.

Psalm 67

Let God arise, Let his enemies be scattered; Let those who hate him flee from before him.

As smoke vanishes, let them vanish: as wax melts before the fire, so let the sinners perish from before God.

But let the righteous rejoice; let them exult before God: let them be delighted with joy.

Sing to God, sing praises to his name: make a way for him that ascended into the west (the Lord is his name) and exult before him. They shall be troubled before his face;

He is the father of the orphans and judge of the widows: such is God in his holy place.

God settles the solitary in a house; leading forth prisoners mightily, also those who act provokingly, even those who dwell in tombs.

O God when you went forth before your people when you went through the wilderness;

The earth quaked, yes, the heavens dropped at the presence of the God of Sinai, at the presence of the God of Israel.

O God, you will grant to your inheritance a gracious rain; for it was weary, but you did refresh it.

Your creatures dwell in it: you have in your goodness prepared for the poor.

The Lord God will give a word to those who preach the good news in much power.

The king of the powers of the beloved, even in the beauty of the house divides the spoils.

Even if you should lie among the lots, you shall have the wings of a dove covered with silver and her chest with yellow gold.

When the heavenly One scatters kings upon it, they shall be made snow-white in Selmon.

The mountain of God is a rich mountain; a swelling mountain, a rich mountain.

Why then do you conceive evil, you swelling mountains? This is the mountain which God has delighted to dwell in; yes, the Lord will dwell in it for ever.

The chariots of God are ten thousand fold, thousands of rejoicing ones: the Lord is among them, in Sinai, in the holy place.

You have gone up on high, you have led captivity captive, you have received gifts for man, yes, for they were rebellious, that you might dwell among them. Blessed be the Lord God, blessed be the Lord every day; and the God of our salvation shall prosper us.

Our God is the God of salvation; and to the Lord belong the escape from death.

But God will shatter the heads of his enemies; the hairy crown of those who go on in their trespasses.

The Lord said: I will bring them again from Basan, I will bring my people again through the depths of the sea.

That your foot may be dipped in blood and the tongue of your dogs be stained with that of your enemies.

Your goings, O God, have been seen; the goings of my God, the king, in the sanctuary.

The princes went first, next before the players on instruments, in the midst of young women playing on timbrels.

Praise God in the congregations, the Lord from the fountains of Israel.

There is Benjamin the younger one in ecstasy, the princes of Juda their rulers, the princes of Zabulon, the princes of Nephthali.

O God, command your strength: strengthen, O God, what you have accomplished in us.

Because of your temple at Jerusalem shall kings bring presents to you.

Rebuke the wild beasts of the reed: let the crowd of bulls with the heifers of the nations be rebuked, so that they who have been proved with silver may not be shut out: scatter the nations that wish for wars.

Ambassadors shall arrive out of Egypt; Ethiopia shall hasten to stretch out her hand to God.

Sing to God, you kingdoms of the earth; sing psalms to the Lord. Sing to God that has ascended upon the heaven of heaven, eastward: Behold, he will utter a mighty sound with his voice.

Give glory to God: his excellency is over Israel and his power is in the clouds.

God is wonderful in his holy places, the God of Israel: he will give power and strength to his people: blessed be God.

Psalm 68

Save me, O God; for the waters have come in to my soul.

I am stuck fast in deep mire and there is no standing: I have descended to the depths of the sea and a storm has overwhelmed me.

I am weary of crying, my throat has become hoarse; my eyes have failed by my waiting on my God.

Those who hate me without a cause are more than the hairs of my head: the enemies that persecute me unrighteously are strengthened: then I restored that which I took not away.

O God, you know my foolishness; and my transgressions are not hidden from you.

Let not those who wait on you, O Lord of Hosts, be ashamed on my account: let not those who seek you, be ashamed on my account, O God of Israel.

For I have suffered reproach for your sake; shame has covered my face.

I became a foreigner to my brothers and a stranger to my mother's children.

For the zeal of your house has eaten me up; and the reproaches of those who reproached you are fallen upon me.

I bowed down my soul with fasting and that was made my reproach.

I put on sackcloth for my covering; and I became a proverb to them.

Those who sit in the gate talked against me and those who drank wine sang against me.

But I will cry to you, O Lord, in my prayer; O God, it is a propitious time: in the multitude of your mercy hear me, in the truth of your salvation.

Save me from the mire, that I may not be lost in it: let me be delivered from those who hate me and from the deep waters.

Let not the water flood drown me, nor let the deep swallow me up; neither let the well shut its mouth upon me.

Hear me, O Lord; for your mercy is good: according to the multitude of your compassions look upon me.

And turn not away your face from your servant; for I am afflicted: hear me speedily.

Draw near to my soul and redeem it: deliver me because of my enemies.

For you know my reproach and my shame and my confusion; all that afflict me are before you.

My soul has waited for reproach and misery; and I waited for one to grieve with me, but there was none; and for one to comfort me, but I found none.

They gave me also gall for my food and made me drink vinegar for my thirst.

Let their table before them be for a snare and for a recompense and for a stumbling-block.

Let their eyes be darkened that they should not see; and bow down their back continually.

Pour out your wrath upon them, Let the fury of your anger take hold on them.

Let their habitation be made desolate; Let there be no inhabitant in their tents:

Because they persecuted him whom you have stricken;and they have added to the grief of my wounds.

Add iniquity to their iniquity; Let them not come into your righteousness.

Let them be blotted out of the book of the living, let them not be written with the righteous.

I am poor and sorrowful; but the salvation of your countenance has helped me.

I will praise the name of my God with a song, I will magnify him with praise;

And this shall please God more than a young calf having horns and hoofs.

Let the poor see and rejoice; seek the Lord diligently and you shall live.

For the Lord hears the poor and does not set at nought his fettered ones.

Let the heavens and the earth raise him, the sea and all things moving in them.

For God will save Zion and the cities of Judea shall be built; men shall dwell there and inherit it.

The descendants of his servants shall possess it and those who love his name shall dwell in it.

Instead of the Prayer of Saint Basil, on Saturdays we say this…

Prayer of Saint Efstratios

I magnify you greatly, O Lord, because you have looked upon my lowliness, and have not hemmed me into the hands of enemies, but have saved my soul from constraints. And now, Master, let your hand protect me, and your mercy come upon me, for my soul has been troubled and is greatly afflicted at its departure from this wretched and soiled body of mine. May the evil plan of the adversary never confront and obstruct it, because of the many sins committed by me in this life in knowledge and in ignorance. Be merciful to me, Master, and never let my soul see the dark and gloomy sight of the evil demons; but may your bright and shining Angels receive it. Give glory to your holy name, and bring me by your power to your divine judgment seat. When I am judged, let not the hand of the ruler of this world seize me to cast me, sinner that I am, into the depths of Hell; but stand by me and be for me a savior and a helper. Have mercy, Lord, on my soul, stained with the passions of life, and receive it pure through repentance and confession; for you are blessed to the ages of ages. Amen.

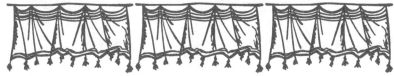

The Lightgiver

SERVICE OF PREPARATION FOR HOLY COMMUNION

AT COMPLINE

When you intend to approach the most pure Mysteries, during Compline (p. 43), at the end of the Creed, say with compunction the following Canon, whose acrostic in Greek is the alphabet.

THE CANON

Ode 1. Mode 2. Come, you peoples.

Compassionate Lord, may your holy Body become for me the Bread of everlasting life, and your precious Blood a remedy for sicknesses of every kind.

Defiled by foul deeds, wretch that I am, I am unworthy, O Christ, of participation in your most pure Body and your divine Blood. Make me worthy of it.

Theotokion.

Blessed Bride of God, good earth which put forth the un-husbanded Ear of Corn that saved the world, make me, who eat it, worthy to be saved.

Ode 3. You have established me.

Grant me showers of tears, O Christ, to purify the filth of my heart, so that cleansed and with a good conscience I may draw near, Master, with faith and fear at the Communion of your divine Gifts.

May your most pure Body and your divine Blood, Lover of mankind, bring me pardon of faults, communion of the Holy Spirit, eternal life, and removal of passions and tribulations.

Theotokion.

All-holy table of the Bread of life, which through mercy came down from on high and gives new life to the world, now make me too, who am unworthy, worthy to take it with fear and to live.

Ode 4. You have come from a Virgin.

Made flesh, for our sake, O most merciful, you were willing to be sacrificed like a sheep for the sins of mortals. Therefore I implore you to wipe away my offenses also.

Heal the wound of my soul, Lord, sanctify me wholly, and count me worthy, Master, to partake of your mystical divine Supper, wretch though I am.

Theotokion.

For me too, Sovereign Lady, appease the One who came from your womb, and keep me, your suppliant, undefiled and blameless, so that, as I receive the spiritual pearl, I may be sanctified.

Ode 5. The giver of light.

As you foretold, O Christ, so may it be for your poor servant, and abide in me as you promised; for see, I eat your divine Body and I drink your Blood.

Word of God and God, may the burning coal of your Body bring enlightenment to me who am in darkness, and your Blood cleansing of my defiled soul.

Theotokion.

Mary, Mother of God, the honored tabernacle of the sweet fragrance, by your prayers make me a vessel of election, that I may share in the holy gifts of your Offspring.

Ode 6. Encompassed by an abyss.

O Savior, sanctify my mind, soul, heart, and body, and count me worthy, Master, to draw near, without condemnation, to your dread Mysteries.

May I be made a stranger to passions and obtain increase of grace and assurance of life through the communion of your holy Mysteries, O Christ.

Theotokion.

O God, the holy Word of God, at the intercessions of your holy Mother, sanctify me wholly who now draws near to your divine Mysteries.

Kontakion. Tone 2. Seeking things on high.

Do not disdain, O Christ, to let me now receive the Bread, your Body, and your divine Blood, and may my partaking of your most pure and dread Mysteries, wretch that I am, not be for my condemnation. But may it be for me for eternal and immortal life.

Ode 7. When the golden image.

May the Communion of your immortal Mysteries, O Christ, only loving Protector, now be for me the source of good things: of light and life, dispassion, and progress in more godly virtue, and of blessing, that I may glorify you.

May I be delivered from passions, enemies, constraints, and every tribulation as, with trembling and love, and with devotion, lover of mankind, I now approach your immortal and divine Mysteries, and sing to you: Blessed are you the God of our fathers.

Theotokion.

O full of God's grace, who beyond understanding gave birth to the Savior Christ, I, your servant, in my impurity entreat you in your purity, make me, who am now about to draw near to the most pure Mysteries, wholly pure of defilement of flesh and spirit.

Ode 8. The God who in the furnace of fire.

Christ, God, my Savior, even in my despair, count me also, worthy now to be a partaker in your heavenly, dread, and holy Mysteries, and your divine and mystical Supper.

As I take refuge under your compassion, O Good One, I cry to you in fear: Abide in me, my Savior, and may I, as you said, abide in you. For see, confident in your mercy, I eat your Body and I drink your Blood.

Theotokion.

I shudder as I receive the fire. May I not be burned up like wax, like grass. O fearful Mystery! O divine compassion!

How can I , who am clay, partake of your divine Body and Blood and be made incorruptible?

Ode 9. The Son of the Father who has no beginning.

In it Christ the Lord: taste and see. For he of old became like us for our sake, and having offered himself once as an oblation to his own Father, he is ever slain, and sanctifies those who partake.

In soul and body, Master, may I be sanctified, enlightened, saved. May I become your house by participation in your sacred Mysteries, and have you dwell in me, with the Father and the Spirit, most merciful Benefactor.

May your Body and most precious Blood be to me as fire and light, my Savior, consuming the matter of my sins, burning up the thorns of passions, and enlightening me wholly, that I may worship your Godhead.

Theotokion.

God was embodied from your pure blood; therefore every generation sings your praise; Sovereign Lady. The multitudes of spiritual beings glorify you, for through you they see clearly the one who is Master of all things endowed with human nature.

And immediately It is truly right. *Trisagion.* Glory. Both Now. All Holy Trinity. Lord, have mercy *(x3).* Glory. Both Now. Our Father. For yours is. *and then the rest of Compline, see pg. 50.*

ON THE NEXT MORNING

After the usual morning prayers, say:

The Trisagion... Glory. Both now. All Holy Trinity...Lord, have mercy *(x3)* Glory. Both now. Our Father...For yours is...Lord have mercy *(x12)* Glory. Both Now. Come let us worship...*(x3) and the following Psalms.*

Psalm 22

The Lord shepherds me, and I shall lack nothing. He has settled me in a place of green pasture. He has reared me by the water of rest. He has turned my soul back. He has led me on paths of justice, for his name's sake. For even if I walk in the midst of the shadow of death, I will not fear evils, for you are with me. Your rod and your staff have comforted me. You have prepared a table before me in the face of those who afflict me. You have anointed my head with oil and your cup inebriates me like the strongest wine. Your mercy will follow me all the days of my life.

Psalm 23

The earth is the Lord's and all that is in it, the whole world and all who dwell in it. For he founded it upon seas and made it ready upon rivers. Who will ascend into the mount of the Lord, and who will stand in his Holy Place? Those whose hands are innocent and who are pure in heart, who have not given their souls to vanity nor sworn deceitfully to their neighbor. They will receive blessings from the Lord, and mercy from God their Savior. This is the generation of those that seek the Lord, that seek the face of the God of Jacob. Lift up your gates you rulers; and be lifted up you eternal gates, and the King of glory will come in. Who is this King of glory? The mighty and powerful Lord, the Lord powerful in war. Lift up your gates you rulers; and be lifted up your eternal gates, and the King of glory will come in. Who is this King of glory? The Lord of powers, he is the King of glory.

Psalm 115

I believed, therefore I spoke; but I was greatly humbled. But I said in my amazement: Every human is a liar. What return shall I make to the Lord for all that he has given me in my turn? I will take the Cup of salvation, and I will call on the name of the Lord. I will pay my vows to the Lord, in the sight of all his people. Precious in the sight of the Lord is the death of his holy one. Lord, I am your servant, your servant and child of your handmaid. You have torn apart my bonds. I will sacrifice a sacrifice of praise to you, and I will call on the name of the Lord. I will pay my vows to the Lord in the sight of all his people, in the courts of the house of the Lord, in your midst, O Jerusalem.

Glory to the Father, and to the Son, and to the Holy Spirit. Both now and ever and to the ages of ages. Amen. Alleluia (x3). Glory to you, O God. Lord, have mercy. (x3).

And the following Troparia. Mode 6.

Lord, born from a Virgin overlook my iniquities and purify my heart, making it a temple of your most pure Body and Blood. You, whose mercy is without measure, do not cast me away from your presence.

Glory to the Father and the Son and the Holy Spirit.

How do I, the unworthy, have the rashness to receive Communion of your Sanctifying Gifts? For should I dare approach with those who are worthy, my garment convicts me, for it is not that of the Supper, and I would procure condemnation for my most sinful soul. Purify the filth of my soul, Lord, and save me, for you love mankind.

Both now and forever and to the ages of ages. Amen.

Theotokion.

Many are the multitudes of my failings, Mother of God. To you I come for refuge, pure Virgin, asking for salvation. Visit my sick soul, and intercede with your Son and our God that I may be given forgiveness for the dreadful deeds I have done, O only blessed one.

But on Holy and Great Thursday, the following:

When the glorious Disciples were enlightened at the Supper by the washing of the feet, then Judas, the ungodly, sick from avarice, was darkened and delivered you, the just Judge, to lawless judges. Look, lover of money, at the one who hanged himself because of it. Flee from that insatiable soul, which dared such things against his Teacher. Lord, loving towards all, glory to you.

Then, Lord, have mercy. *(x40). As many prostrations as you wish, and immediately the following Prayers of Supplication.*

VERSES OF INSTRUCTION

On how one should approach
the most pure Mysteries.
Symeon Metaphrastes

When you are going to eat the Master's body,
Draw near with fear, lest you be burned: 'tis fire.
And when you drink God's blood to share in him,
With those who grieve you first be reconciled,
And then with boldness eat the mystic food.

Other similar verses.

Before you share in the dread sacrifice
Of the life-giving body of the Master,
With fear and trembling make your prayer like this:

1ˢᵗ Prayer

By Saint Basil the Great

Master, Lord Jesus Christ our God, the source of Life and immortality, maker of all creation, visible and invisible, the co-eternal and co-everlasting Son of the everlasting Father in the abundance of your goodness you put on flesh in these last days, were crucified and slain for us, ungrateful and thankless though we are, and with your own blood you refashioned our nature, which had been corrupted by sin. Accept, immortal King, the repentance even of me, a sinner; incline your ear to me and hearken to my words. I have sinned, Lord, I have sinned against heaven and before you, and I am not worthy to gaze on the height of your glory. I have angered your goodness by transgressing your commandments and not obeying your ordinances. But, Lord, since you are forbearing, long-suffering, and full of mercy, you have not handed me over to be destroyed along with my iniquities, but have constantly waited for my conversion. For you said, through your prophet, O Lover of mankind, I in no way desire the death of the sinner, but rather that he be converted and live. For you do not want the work of your hands to perish. Master, nor do you take pleasure in the destruction of mortals, but you want all to be saved and come to knowledge of the truth. And so I too, though I am unworthy of heaven and earth and of this transient life ófor I have made myself wholly subject to sin, have become enslaved to pleasures, and defiled your image but am nevertheless your creature and your handiwork–do not despair of my salvation, wretch though I am, but made bold by your measureless compassion I draw near. Receive me also, O Christ, lover of mankind, as you received the Harlot, the Thief, the Publican, and the Prodigal. Take away the heavy burden of my sins, you who take away the sin of the world and heal the infirmities of humankind; who call to yourself those who toil and are heavy laden and give them rest; who did not come to call the just, but sinners to repentance. Cleanse me of all defilement of flesh and spirit; teach me to achieve perfect holiness by fear of you, so that receiving a share of your holy gifts with the witness of my conscience clean, I may be united to your holy Body and Blood and have you dwelling and abiding in me, with the Father and your Holy Spirit. Yes, Lord Jesus Christ my God, may the communion of your most pure and life-giving Mysteries not be to me for judgment; may I not become weak in soul and body from partaking of them unworthily; but grant me, until my last breath, to receive without condemnation a share of your sanctifying gifts, for communion of the Holy Spirit, provision for the journey to eternal life, and an acceptable defense at your dread judgment seat, so that I too, with all your chosen ones, may become a sharer in your pure blessings, which you have prepared for those who love you, Lord, among whom you are glorified to the ages. Amen.

2ⁿᵈ *Prayer*

By the same.

I know, Lord, that I partake unworthily of your most pure Body and your precious blood, that I am guilty and eat and drink judgment to myself, not discerning your Body and Blood, Christ my God; but made bold by your compassion I draw near to you, who said: Those who eat my flesh and drink my blood, abide in me and I in them. Have compassion on me, therefore, Lord, and do not put me, a sinner, to public shame, but deal with me in accordance with your mercy and let these holy things give me healing, cleansing, enlightenment, protection, salvation, and sanctification of soul and body, the averting of every delusion, every wicked deed and activity of the devil, which operates intentionally in my members; may they bring me confidence and love towards you; amendment of life and assurance, increase of virtue and perfection; fulfilling of your commandments; communion of the Holy Spirit; provision for the journey to eternal life, and an acceptable defense at your dread judgment seat; not judgment or condemnation.

3ʳᵈ Prayer

By John Chrysostom.

Lord, my God, I know that I am not fit or worthy for you to come under the roof of the house of my soul because it is wholly desolate and ruined, and you do not have in me a place worthy for you to lay your head. But as you humbled yourself from on high for our sake, do not limit yourself to the measure of my lowliness. And as you accepted to be laid in a cave and a manger of unreasoning beasts, even so consent to enter the manger of my unreasoning soul and my defiled body. And as you did not disdain to go in and sup with sinners in the house of Simon the leper, so consent to enter the house of my poor soul, leper and sinner though I am. And as you did not reject the woman who was, like me, harlot and sinner, when she drew near and touched you, so have compassion also on me, a sinner, as I draw near and touch you. And as you did not abhor her filthy and polluted mouth when it kissed you, do not abhor my even filthier and more polluted mouth, nor my foul, unclean and sordid lips, and my yet more sordid tongue. But let the burning coal of your all-holy Body and precious Blood bring me sanctification, enlightenment, and strengthening of my humble soul and body; alleviation of the weight of my many offenses; protection against every activity of the devil; averting and hindering of my mean and wicked habits; mortification of the passions; fulfilling of your commandments; an increase of your divine grace, and the attaining of your kingdom. For I do not draw near to you in presumption, Christ my God, but as one who takes courage from your ineffable goodness; and so that I may not, by long absenting myself from communion with you, become prey to the intangible wolf. Therefore I beg you, Master, as you alone are holy, make holy my soul and body, my mind and heart, all my inward parts. Renew the whole of me, root the fear of you in my members, and may your sanctification never be effaced in me. Be my helper and defender, direct my life in peace, and make me worthy of the place at your right hand with your Saints; at the prayers and entreaties of your all-immaculate Mother, of your bodiless, ministering, and immaculate Powers and of all your Saints, who have been well-pleasing to you from every age. Amen.

4th Prayer

By the same.

I am not worthy, Master and Lord, that you should come under the roof of my soul; but since, as you love mankind, you wish to dwell in me, with courage I draw near. You give the command; I will open the gates which you alone created, and you enter with love for mankind, as is your nature; you enter and enlighten my darkened reasoning. I believe that you will do this; for you did not send away the Harlot when she drew near to you with tears, you did not cast out the Publican when he repented, reject the Thief when he acknowledged your kingship, but all those who were brought to you by repentance you ranked in the choir of your friends, you who alone are blessed, always, now, and to the unending ages. Amen.

5th Prayer

By the same.

Lord Jesus Christ my God, absolve, forgive, cleanse, and pardon me, a sinner and your unprofitable and unworthy servant, my failings, faults, and offenses by which I have sinned against you from my youth until this present day and hour, whether in knowledge or ignorance, in words or deeds or thoughts or in intentions and habits and in all my senses. And at the intercession of Mary, your Mother, the all-pure and Ever-Virgin, who conceived you without seed, my only hope that does not disappoint, my protection and salvation, count me worthy to partake uncondemned of your immaculate, immortal, life-giving and dread Mysteries for forgiveness of sins and everlasting life; for sanctification, enlightenment, strength, healing, and health of soul and body; the wiping out and complete disappearance of my wicked thoughts, and desires, and purposes, and night time apparitions of the dark and wicked spirits. For the kingdom, the power, the glory, the honor and the worship are yours, with the Father and the Holy Spirit, now and forever, and to the ages of ages. Amen.

6th Prayer

By Saint John of Damascus.

Master, Lord Jesus Christ our God, who alone have authority to forgive sins; as you are good and love mankind, overlook all my offenses committed in knowledge and in ignorance, and count me worthy without condemnation to partake of your divine, glorious, immaculate and life-giving Mysteries, not for punishment, nor for the increase of my sins, but for cleansing and sanctification and a pledge of the life and kingdom to come, for a wall, help, and routing of adversaries, for the blotting out of my many transgressions. For you are a God of mercy, compassion, and love for mankind, and to you we give glory, with the Father and the Holy Spirit, now and forever, and to the ages of ages. Amen.

7th Prayer

By Symeon the New Theologian.

From filthy lips and from a loathsome heart,
An impure tongue, and a polluted soul
Receive my supplications, O my Christ,
Do not reject my words, my ways, or my
Presumption. Give me confidence to say
The Things that I have wanted to, my Christ;
Or rather, teach me what I ought to do
And say.

More than the Harlot I have sinned.
Who, when she learned where you were staying,
bought Sweet myrrh and came,
with boldness to anoint
Your feet, my Christ, my Master and my God.

But, as you did not drive away the one
Whose heart made me draw near, O Word, do not
Abhor me; rather grant that I may clasp
Your feet, kiss and anoint them boldly with
A stream of tears, as with most precious myrrh.

Wash me with my tears,
O Word, and with them Cleanse me;
forgive my faults and grant me pardon.
You know how many are my evil deeds,
You know my wounds, too, and you see my bruises;
But my faith, too, you know, and you behold
My eagerness; you also hear my groans.

My God, my Maker, my Redeemer, not
One tear escapes you, not one part of one.

Your eyes know all that I have not yet done;
The actions also as yet unperformed
Have been already written in your book.

Look on my lowliness, look on my toil,
How great it is. Forgive me all my sins,
O God of all things, that with a pure heart,
A fearful mind, and with a contrite soul
I may partake of your immaculate
And most pure Mysteries, by which all those
Who eat and drink you with a heart sincere
Are given life and truly deified.

For you have said, my Master:
All who eat My flesh
And drink my blood
Abide in me,
While I am found in them.

The word of my Master and God is true in every way.
For one who shares God's deifying graces
Is not alone, but is with you, my Christ,
The light with triple sun, that lights the world.

And so that I may not remain alone
Apart from you, Giver of life,
My breath, my life,
My joy, salvation of the world,
Because of this I now draw near to you,
As you can see, with tears and contrite heart,
Imploring that I may receive from you
Ransom from all my faults, and uncondemned
Share in your pure, life-giving Mysteries;
That you may, as you said, remain with me,
Most wretched that I am, lest the deceiver
Find me without your grace,
And by his guile
Grab me and
From your deifying words
Lead me astray.

Because of this I fall
Before you, and with fervor cry to you:
As you accepted both the Prodigal
And, when she came to you, the Harlot, so
Accept me, too, harlot and prodigal,
Who now draws near to you with contrite soul.

Savior, I know that none has sinned like me
Against you, none has done the deeds that I
Have done.

But this I also know: neither

The magnitude of my sins exceeds my God's
Forbearance and great love for mankind.
But with the oil of mercy and compassion
All those who fervently repent you cleanse,
Make radiant and let them share your light,
Bounteously making them partakers in
Your Godhead. And, though strange to Angels and
To mortal minds, you often speak with them
As with your own true friends.

This makes me bold,
This gives me wings, my Christ, and confident
In your rich blessings for us, I partake
Of fire, with joy and yet with trembling,
For I am grass, but–wonder strange–
I am refreshed with dew ineffably,
Just as the bush of old was burning but
Yet unconsumed.

Therefore with thankful mind,
With thankful heart, with thankful members of
Both soul and flesh I worship, magnify,
And glorify you, O my God, for you
Are ever blessed now and to the ages.

8th Prayer

By Symeon Metaphrastes.

Lord, alone pure and undefiled, Christ Jesus, Wisdom of God, peace and power, through the inexpressible compassion of your love for mankind you have assumed our whole fabric from the pure and virgin blood of her who conceived you in a manner above nature by the coming of the divine Spirit and the good pleasure of the eternal Father. With the human nature, which you assumed, you accepted the life-giving and saving Passion, the Cross, the Nails, the Lance, Death itself: mortify the soul-destroying passions of my body. By your burial you despoiled the palaces of Hell: bury my wicked intentions through good thoughts, and scatter the spirits of wickedness. By your life-bearing Resurrection on the third day you raised up the fallen Forefathers: raise me up, who have sunk down through sin, by setting before me ways of repentance. By your glorious Ascension you deified the flesh that you assumed, and honored it with the throne at the Father's right hand: count me worthy through the Communion of your holy Mysteries to obtain the portion of the saved at your right hand. By the descent of the Comforter Spirit you made your sacred Disciples his precious vessels: declare me too to be a receptacle of his coming. You are going to come again to judge the whole world with justice: be well pleased for me, my Maker and Fashioner, to go to meet you in the clouds, with all your Saints, so that I may unendingly glorify and sing your praise, with your Father who has no beginning, and your all-holy, good, and life-giving Spirit, now and for ever, and to the ages of ages. Amen.

9th Prayer

By John of Damascus.

I stand before the doors of your Temple yet do not refrain from evil thoughts. But do you, Christ God, who justified the Publican, had mercy on the woman of Canaan, and opened the gates of Paradise to the Thief, open for me the compassion of your love for mankind and receive me as I draw near and touch you, like the Harlot and the woman with an issue of blood. For the one touched your hem and readily received healing, while the other clasped your most pure feet and obtained remission of her sins. But may I, poor wretch, who draw to receive your whole Body, not be burned up; but receive me like them, enlighten the senses of my soul, and burn up the indictment of my sin, at the intercessions of her who have birth to you without seed and of the heavenly Powers; for you are blessed to the ages of ages. Amen.

10th Prayer

By John Chrysostom.

I believe, Lord, and I confess, that you are truly the Christ, the Son of the living God, who came into the world to save sinners, of whom I am the first. Also I believe that this is indeed your most pure Body, and this indeed your precious Blood. Therefore I beseech you, have mercy on me and forgive me my offenses, voluntary and involuntary, in word and in deed, in knowledge and in ignorance, and count me worthy to partake uncondemned of your most pure Mysteries for forgiveness of sins and eternal life. Amen.

As you go to receive Communion,
say the following verses to yourself:

See, to divine Communion I draw near;
My Maker, burn me not as I partake,
For you are fire consuming the unworthy,
But therefore make me clean from every stain.

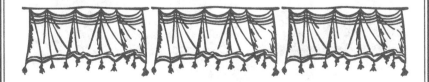

Panagia Faneromeni

THANKSGIVING AFTER HOLY COMMUNION

Verses of Admonition

Whenever you have had Communion
Of the life-giving and transcendent gifts,
At once give praise and offer heartfelt thanks,
And from your soul say fervently to God:
Glory to you, O God, Glory to you, O God,
Glory to you, O God!

And immediately the prayers of thanksgiving:

Anonymous

I thank you, Lord, my God, because you have not rejected me a sinner, but have counted me worthy to be a communicant of your Holy Things. I thank you, because you have counted me, the unworthy, worthy to share in your most pure and heavenly gifts. But, Master, Lover of mankind, who died for our sake and rose again, and gave us these your awe-inspiring and life-giving Mysteries, grant that these gifts may bring me also healing of soul and body, the repelling of every adversary, the enlightenment of the eyes of my heart, peace of my spiritual powers, faith unashamed, love without pretense, fullness of wisdom, the keeping of your commandments, increase of your divine grace, and the gaining of your Kingdom; that preserved through them by your sanctification, I may always remember your grace, and no longer live for myself but for you, our Master and Benefactor. And so, when I leave this present life in the hope of life eternal, I shall find everlasting repose where the sound of those who feast is unceasing, and the delight of those who see the ineffable beauty of your face is unbounded. For you are the true desire and the inexpressible joy of those who love you, Christ our God, and all creation hymns you to the ages. Amen.

Basil the Great

Master, Christ God, King of the ages, and Creator of all things, I thank you for all the good things you have given me, and for communion in your most pure and life-giving mysteries. Therefore I pray you, O Good One, Lover of mankind: guard me under your protection and in the shadow of your wings; and grant that until my last breath I may share worthily and with a pure conscience in your holy things for remission of sins and everlasting life. For you are the Bread of life, the source of sanctification, the giver of blessings; and to you we give glory, with the Father and the Holy Spirit, now and for ever, and to the ages of ages. Amen.

Symeon Metaphrastes

You who willing give me your flesh for food,
Who are a fire consuming the unworthy;
Do not burn me up, my Maker;
But penetrate the structure of my limbs,
All my joints, my inner parts, my heart:
Burn up the thorns of all my offenses.

Purify my soul and sanctify my mind.
Strengthen my knees, together with my bones;

Enlighten the five-fold simpleness of my senses;
Nail down the whole of me with fear of you.

Always protect, guard, and keep me
From every soul-destroying deed and word.

Hallow me, purify me, bring me to harmony,
And give me beauty, understanding, light;
Show me to be your dwelling,
the Spirit's house alone,
And no more the dwelling place of sin;
That, by the entrance of Communion,
Every evil-doer, every passion
May flee from me, your house, as from a fire.

As intercessors I bring you all the Saints,
The companies of the Bodiless Hosts,
Your forerunner, the wise Apostles,
And with them your most pure and holy Mother;
Accept their prayers, O my compassionate Christ,
And make your worshiper a child of light.

For you alone are the sanctification of our souls,
O Good One, and their brightness,
And fittingly to you, as to our God and Master,
We all give praise and glory every day.

Anonymous

May your holy Body, Lord Jesus Christ, our God, bring me eternal life, and your precious Blood forgiveness of sins. May this Eucharist bring me joy, health, and gladness; and at your dread Second Coming make me, a sinner, worthy to stand at the right hand of your glory, at the prayers of your all pure Mother and of all your Saints. Amen.

Anonymous. To the All-holy Theotokos.

All-holy Lady, Theotokos, the light of my darkened soul, my hope, protection, refuge, comfort, joy, I thank you, because you have made me, the unworthy, worthy to become a partaker in the most pure Body and precious Blood of your Son. But, O you who gave birth to the true Light, enlighten the spiritual eyes of my heart; you who bore the source of immortality, give life to me, who has been slain by sin; you the compassionate Mother of the merciful God, have mercy on me and give me compunction and contrition in my heart, humility in my ideas, and release from the imprisonment of my thoughts. And count me worthy, until my last breath, to receive without condemnation the sanctification of the most pure Mysteries, for healing of soul and body; and grant me tears of repentance and thanksgiving, to praise and glorify you all the days of my life. For you are blessed and glorified to the ages. Amen.

Now, Master, let your servant depart in peace, according to your word; for my eyes have seen your salvation which you have prepared before the face of all peoples, a light for revelation to the nations, and the glory of your people Israel.

Trisagion.

Holy God, Holy Mighty, Holy Immortal, have mercy on us (*x3*).

Glory to the Father, and the Son, and the Holy Spirit, now and forever and to the ages of ages. Amen.

All-holy Trinity, have mercy on us. Lord, forgive our sins. Master, pardon our transgressions. Holy One, visit and heal our infirmities for the glory of Your name.

Lord, have mercy. *(x3)* Glory to the Father, and the Son, and the Holy Spirit, now and forever and to the ages of ages. Amen.

Our Father, who art in heaven, hallowed be Thy name. Thy kingdom come. Thy will be done, on earth as it is in heaven. Give us this day our daily bread; and forgive us our trespasses, as we forgive those who trespass against us. And lead us not into temptation, but deliver us from the evil one.

Through the prayers of our Holy Fathers, Lord Jesus Christ our God, have mercy on us and save us. Amen.

The Apolytikion of the day, to Theotokion, of the Church and the Apolytikion and Kontakion of Saint John Chrysostom or Basil the Great.

Apolytikion of the Sacred Chrysostom. Mode 8.

The grace which shone from your mouth like a torch of flame enlightened the whole earth; it laid up for the world the treasures of freedom from avarice; it showed us the height of humility. But as you train us by your words, Father John Chrysostom, intercede with Christ God, the Word, that our souls may be saved.

Kontakion of the Sacred Chrysostom.
Mode 6. When you had fulfilled.

You received divine grace from heaven, and through your lips you teach us all to worship one God in Trinity, venerable John Chrysostom, wholly blessed. Fittingly we praise you, for you are a teacher who makes clear things divine.

And:

At the prayers of all your Saints and of the Mother of God, grant us your peace, O Lord, and have mercy on us, for you alone are compassionate.

If it is a Despotic or Theometoric feast, say the first Apolytikion of the feast, then that of the sacred Chrysostom or Basil the Great, and then:

Lord, have mercy *(x12)*. Glory to the Father, and the Son, and the Holy Spirit, now and forever and to the ages of ages. Amen.

Greater in honor than the Cherubim, and beyond compare more glorious than the Seraphim, without corruption, you gave birth to God the Word; truly the Theotokos, we magnify you.

Glory to the Father, and the Son, and the Holy Spirit, now and forever and to the ages of ages. Amen.

Lord, have mercy *(x3)*.

Through the prayers of our Holy Fathers, Lord Jesus Christ our God, have mercy on us and save us. Amen.

"Most assuredly, I say to you, unless you eat the flesh of the Son of Man and drink His blood, you have no life in you. Whoever eats My flesh and drinks My blood has eternal life..." (John 6:53-54)

THE PRAYER OF THE HEART

ON THE INVOCATION OF THE NAME

From *The Way of the Spirit: Reflections on Life in God*,
Archimandrite Aimilianos of Simonopetra, Mount Athos

translated by Maximos Simonopetrites

Lord Jesus Christ,
Son of God, have mercy on me.

Κύριε Ἰησοῦ Χριστέ,
Υἱὲ τοῦ Θεοῦ, ἐλέησόν με.

Many theologians ask themselves: "Am I truly a theologian? Am I worthy of being a theologian?…St. Neilos tells them: "If you pray truly, you are a theologian."

In speaking of prayer, St. Neilos, like all the Fathers, speaks of *the* prayer, namely: the Prayer of the Heart. This is the ceaseless invocation of the name of Jesus, the unbroken contemplation of God through Christ. Whether I want to or not, whether I am able to or not, the Prayer of the Heart will bring me understanding, and as soon as I say: "Lord Jesus Christ," it will bring me the Lord Himself, for it is His name, His form, and His glory, that are enfolded in the words of this prayer.

Just as a child within its mother's womb kicks and makes its presence known, so too does God move about within me. Sometimes He makes my eyes sparkle with joy, and sometimes he fills them with tears. Sometimes I cry aloud, and other times I say to myself: "Lord Jesus Christ, have mercy on me." It is prayer, then, and the Jesus Prayer in particular, that makes us theologians.

St. Basil says that "the soul, through its ardent contemplation and love of God, is made worthy of the gift of theology by the power of God Himself, who enables the eyes of the soul to see all that they desire." My invocation of the name of Jesus is my "ardent contemplation and love of God." It means that I speak to God all the time, simple and naturally, in a filial and friendly way. And as the eyes of my heart are turned to God, He gives me "the gift of theology," He "enables the eyes of my soul to see all that they desire." Theology, then, is a living experience of the uncreated energies of God.

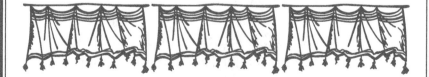

OCCASIONAL PRAYERS

OTHER MORNING PRAYERS

Prayer of Archimandrite Sophrony for Daybreak

O Lord Eternal and Creator of all things, Who of Your inscrutable goodness called me to this life; Who bestowed on me the grace of Baptism and the Seal of the Holy Spirit; Who imbued me with the desire to seek You, the one true God: Hear my prayer. I have no life, no light, no joy or wisdom, no strength except in You, O God. Because of my unrighteousness, I dare not raise my eyes to You. But You said to Your disciples, 'Whatever you shall ask in prayer believing, you shall receive.' and 'Whatever you shall ask in my name, that will I do.' For this reason I dare to invoke You. Purify me from all taint of flesh and spirit. Teach me to pray aright. Bless this day which You have given me, Your unworthy servant. By the power of Your blessing enable me at all times to speak and act to Your glory with a pure spirit, with humility, patience, love, gentleness, peace, courage and wisdom, aware always of Your presence. Of Your immense goodness, O Lord God, show me the path of Your will, and grant me to walk in Your sight without sin. O Lord, unto Whom all hearts are open, You have what I need. You are acquainted with my blindness and my ignorance, You know my weaknesses and my soul's corruption; But neither are my pain and anguish hidden from You. Therefore I beseech You, hear my prayer and by Your Holy Spirit, teach me the way in which I should walk; and when my perverted will would lead me down other paths, spare me, O Lord, and force me back to You. By the power of Your love, grant me to hold fast to that which is good. Preserve me from every word or deed that corrupts the soul; from every impulse unpleasing in Your sight and hurtful to my brethren. Teach me what I should say and how I should speak. If it be Your will that I make no answer, inspire me to keep silent in a spirit of peace that causes neither sorrow nor hurt to my fellow man. Establish me in the path of Your commandments and to my last breath let me not stray from the light of Your ordinances, that Your commandments may become the sole law of my being on this earth and all eternity. Yes, Lord, I pray to You, have pity on me. Spare me in my affliction and my misery and do not hide the way of salvation from me. In my foolishness, O God, I plead with You for many and great things. Yet am I ever mindful of my wickedness, my baseness, my vileness. Have mercy upon me. Do not cast me away from your presence because of my presumption. Rather, increase in me this presumption, and grant to me, the worst of men, to love You as You have commanded, with all my heart, and with all my soul, and with all my mind, and with all my strength: With my whole being. Yes, Lord, by Your Holy Spirit, teach me good judgment and knowledge. Grant me to know Your truth before I go down into the grave. Maintain my life in this world until I may offer You worthy repentance. Take me not away in the midst of my days, nor while my mind is still blind. When You wish to bring my life to an end, forewarn me that I may prepare my soul to come before You. Be with me, O Lord, at that dread hour and grant me the joy of salvation. Cleanse me from secret faults, from all iniquity that is hidden in me; and give me a right answer before Your judgment-seat— Yes, Lord, of Your great mercy and immeasurable love for mankind. Amen.

Morning Prayer of Metropolitan Philaret

Grant, O Lord, that I may face all that this new day is to bring with peace of mind. Grant that I may dedicate my-self completely to Your holy will. For every hour of this day, in-struct and support me in all things. Whatsoever I may receive during the day, teach me to accept them tranquilly, with the firm conviction that everything comes by Your holy will. Govern my thoughts and feelings in all I do and say. When unfore-seen things occur, do not let me forget that everything comes from You. Teach me to behave sincerely and wisely toward every member of my family, not embittering or embarrassing others. Grant me strength, my Lord, to bear the fatigue of the coming day and all that it shall bring. Guide my will and teach me to pray, to believe, to hope, to suffer, to forgive, and to love, and pray Yourself in me. Amen.

PRAYERS FOR ONESELF

Prayer of Saint Dimitri of Rostov

Open, O doors and bolts of my heart, that Christ the King of Glory may enter! Enter, O my Light, and enlighten my darkness; Enter, O my Life, and resurrect my deadness; Enter, O my Physician, and heal my wounds; Enter, O Divine Fire, and burn up the thorns of my sins; Ignite my inward parts and my heart with the flame of Your love; Enter, O my King, and destroy in me the kingdom of sin; Sit on the throne of my heart and alone reign in me, O You, my King and Lord! Amen.

Lord, I do not know what to ask of You. You alone know what I need. You love me more than I am able to love You. Father, give Your servant that for which I am unable to ask. I do not dare to ask either for a cross or for consolation: I only stand before You. My heart is open to You, and You Yourself see needs of which I am unaware. See and do according to Your mercy. Strike me and heal me; knock me down and lift me up. I show reverence and keep silence before Your holy will: Your destiny for me is beyond understanding. I offer myself as a sacrifice to You. I have no other desire besides the desire to carry out Your will. Teach me how to pray – and You Yourself pray in me! Amen.

Prayer for Repentance

God, my good and loving Lord, I acknowledge all the sins which I have committed every day in my life, whether in thought, word or deed. I ask for forgiveness from the depths of my heart for offending You and others and repent of my old ways. Help me by Your grace to change, to sin no more and to walk in the way of righteousness and to praise and glorify Your Name, Father, Son and Holy Spirit. Amen.

PRAYERS FOR LOVED ONES

A Mother's Prayer for Her Children

Holy Father, Immortal, from whom all goodness and gentleness comes, penitently I pray to You for the children whom You have given me to bear. Keep them in Your grace and holiness, that Your name may be glorified in them. Direct me by Your grace to raise them toward the glory of Your holy name and the benefit of other people. Grant me the gift of the patience necessary to do so. O Lord, enlighten the mind of my children with Your Wisdom to learn to love You in their souls and thoughts. Instill in their hearts the fear and abhorrence of every vice, that they may be able to go the right way without sin. Adorn their souls with purity, goodness, humility, diligence, patience, and every virtue. Guard their lips from all slander and lies. Bless my children, that they may progress in virtue and holiness, and grow under Your care into honest people. May their guardian angels be with them and protect them in their youth from misleading thoughts, from the evil and sinful temptations of this world, and from the traps of all unclean spirits. And when my children sin before You, do not turn away Your face from them, but according to Your great mercy be merciful to them, for You alone are the one who cleanses people from all sin. Reward my children with worldly good things and everything they need for salvation. Keep them from wrath, anger, misfortune, evil, and suffering all the days of their lives. O good Lord, I pray to You, grant me joy and happiness from my children. Keep me in righteousness and justice, that with Your children I may stand before You in the day of Your dreaded judgment, and that without fear I may say: Here I am, Lord, with the children whom You have given me, that together with them I may praise Your most holy name of the Father and Son and Holy Spirit, to ages of ages. Amen.

Prayer for One's Sibling(s)

O Lord Jesus Christ, our sweet Savior, Who commanded us, saying, Love one another, even as I have loved you, kindle in my whole being the holy flame of love of You and my neighbor, that in all things I may do Thy will.

O holy Lord, keep also my brother(s) and sister(s) ever in this holy love. Grant them wisdom, health, a good life, and Your Divine grace, so that they may walk in Your ways and do those things that are well-pleasing to You. O sweetest Lord Jesus, help us by Your grace, so that from this time until the end of our life we may love one another, for What is more good and more beautiful than for brothers to live together in unity? Thus, O Lord, hear our prayer and be merciful unto us.

For You are a good God, merciful and You love mankind, and to You do we offer up glory, to the Father, and to the Son, and to the Holy Spirit, both now and ever and unto ages of ages. Amen.

Prayer for a Married Couple

O Merciful God, we beseech You ever to remind us that the married state is holy, and that we must keep it so; Grant us Your grace, that we may continue in faithfulness and love; Increase in us the spirit of mutual understanding and trust, that no quarrel or strife may come between us; Grant us Your blessings, that we may stand before our brethren and in Your sight as an ideal family; And finally, by Your mercy, account us worthy of everlasting life: For You are our sanctification, and to Your we offer up glory, to the Father and to the Son and to the Holy Spirit, now and ever and unto ages of ages. Amen.

Prayer for a Married Couple by Archim. Nicodim (Mandita)

O Lord Jesus Christ our God, our Sweet Savior, Who taught us to always pray for one another, so that by fulfilling your holy law we will be made worthy of Your mercy: look down with compassion on our married life and keep from all perilous falls, from enemies both visible and invisible, my *hus-*

band/wife whom You have given me, that we may pass our time together until the end with oneness of mind. Grant *him/ her* health, strength, and fullness of wisdom enlightened from above, so that *he/she* may be able to fulfill *his/her* duties all the days of this life according to Your will and commandments. Protect and keep *him/her* from temptations, and may *he/she* be able to bear and conquer those temptations that come upon *him/her*. Strengthen *him/her* in right faith, strong hope, and perfect love, so that together we may do good deeds and that we may order all our life according to Your divine ordinances and commandments.

O Greatly-Merciful Lord, hear us who humbly pray to You, and send Your divine blessing in truth on our married life and on all our good deeds, for it is Yours to hear and have mercy on us, O our God, and to You we offer up glory: to the Father and to the Son and to the Holy Spirit, both now and ever, and unto ages of ages. Amen.

Prayer for a Woman with Child

Sovereign Lord Jesus Christ our God, the Source of life and immortality, I thank You, for in my marriage You have blessed me to be a recipient of Your blessing and gift; for You, O Master, said: Be fruitful and multiply and replenish the earth.

I thank You and pray: Bless this fruit of my body that was given to me by You; favor it and animate it by Your Holy Spirit, and let it grow a healthy and pure body, with well-formed limbs.

Sanctify its body, mind, heart, and organs, and grant this infant that is to be born an intelligent soul; establish him in the fear of You.

A faithful angel, a guardian of soul and body, grant unto him. Protect, keep, strengthen, and shelter the child in my womb until the hour of his birth. But conceal him not in his mother's womb; You gave him life and health.

O Lord Jesus Christ, into Your almighty and paternal hands do I entrust my child. Place him upon the right hand of Your grace, and through Your Holy Spirit sanctify him and renew him unto life everlasting, that he may be a communicant of Your Heavenly Kingdom. Amen.

Another Prayer for a Woman with Child

All-Merciful Christ our God, look down and protect me, Your handmaiden, from fear and from evil spirits that seek to destroy the work of Your hands. And when my hour and time is come, deliver me by Your grace.

Look with compassionate eye and deliver me, Your handmaiden, from pain. Lighten my infirmity in the time of my travail and grant me fortitude and strength for birth giving, and hasten it by Your almighty help.

For this is Your glorious work, the power of Your omnipotence, the work of Your grace and tenderheartedness. Amen.

Prayer of Intercession to the Theotokos for a Woman with Child

My most gracious Queen, my hope, O Mother of God, the joy of those in sorrow, help me, for I am helpless.

Intercede and pray to Your Son, Christ our God, that He lighten for me this season while I am with child, and that He ease the burden of heaviness of me, this unworthy handmaiden, and bestow His blessings upon the child to which I am giving birth.

For I know no other help save you, no other hope save you, O Mother of God that will guard and protect me and my child. For by your intercession and help we send up glory and thanksgiving for all things unto the One God in Trinity, the Creator of all, now and ever, and unto the ages of ages. Amen.

Prayer of a Child for His Parents

Our Father, who art in heaven, bless my father and mother, my guardians, and those who are in authority over me, for their love and tender care for me, and for the benefits I receive at their hands.

Help me, I pray, to be respectful and obedient toward them in all things according to Your will, and give me Your grace to perform all of my duties carefully and faithfully, to avoid undesirable company and influence, and to resist all temptation that may come my way; that I may live a sober, righteous and godly life, ever praising You, and glorifying Your holy name. Amen.

Prayer of a Child for His Parents by Archim. Nicodim

O All-Good Lord God, Who granted me good parents, that through them I may become a sharer in many good things; O You Who wills that I should be thankful to them for the life You have given to me through them and for all the care they have had and still have for me, I pray to You with humility for their health and salvation, O God, Who are All-Compassionate, but also All-Righteous, Who blesses children for their parents, but often by Your right hand punishes them for their sins. Receive my humble thanksgiving for the good things which You have poured forth unceasingly on my parents. Send them Your blessings also in the future, O All-Good Master, and forgive all the sins which they may have committed, being human. Teach me to honor in them Your strength, and to be grateful and thankful to them for the life which You have given to me through them, and for all the cares which they have had and still have for me. Help me to follow Your holy commandments, so that I may be submissive and obedient to them, and so that I may do nothing which embitters and saddens them. Reward them, O Most Good One, with Your goodness, for the love and unsleeping care which they always have for me. Protect them from all misfortunes and sorrows. Grant them a long, blessed, quiet and peaceful life. Make them partakers in the blessedness of Your Saints, multiply the fruits of their labors, make Your goodness overflow upon them, that they may increase both in virtues and material abundance, that we may bless You all the days of our lives. Amen.

PRAYERS FOR THE DEPARTED

General Prayer for the Dead

Christ our eternal King and God, You have destroyed death and the devil by Your Cross and have restored man to life by Your Resurrection; give rest, Lord, to the soul of Your servant *(name)* who has fallen asleep, in Your Kingdom, where there is no pain, sorrow or suffering. In Your goodness and love for all men, pardon all the sins *he/she* has committed in thought word or deed, for there is no person who lives and does not sin, You alone are without sin.

For You are the Resurrection, the Life, and Repose of Your servant *(name)*, departed this life, O Christ our God; and to You do we send up glory with Your Eternal Father and Your All-holy, Good and Life-creating Spirit; both now and forever and to the ages of ages. Amen.

Prayer for a Dead Child

O Lord who watches over children in the present life and in the world to come because of their simplicity and innocence of mind, abundantly satisfying them with a place in Abraham's bosom, bringing them to live in radiantly shining places where the spirits of the righteous dwell: receive in peace the soul of Your servant *(name)*, for You Yourself have said, "Let the little children come to Me, for such is the Kingdom of Heaven." Amen.

PRAYERS BEFORE ANY TASK

Almighty God, our Help and Refuge, who knows that we can do nothing right without Your guidance and help; direct me by Your wisdom and power, that I may accomplish this task and, whatever I do according to Your divine will, so that it may be beneficial to me and others and to the glory of Your holy Name. Amen.

Another Prayer

My Lord and Savior, You became man and labored with Your hands until the time of Your ministry. Bless me as I begin this work. Help me to bring it to completion. Lord, enlighten my mind and strengthen my body, that I may accomplish my task according to Your will. Guide me to bring about works of goodness to Your service and glory. Amen.

PRAYERS FOR THOSE IN DISTRESS

Prayer for Those Depressed

O my beloved Queen, my hope, O Mother of God, protector of orphans and protector of those who are hurt, the savior of those who perish, and the consolation of all who are in distress: You see my misery, my sorrow and my loneliness. Help me; I am powerless. Give me strength. You know what I suffer, You know my grief. Lend me Your hand, for who else can be my hope but You, my protector and my intercessor before God? I have sinned before You and before all people. Be my Mother, my consoler, my helper. Protect me and save me; chase grief away from me; chase away my lowness of heart and my despondency. Help me, O Mother of my God! Amen.

Prayer for Mental Well-being

O Master, Lord my God, in Whose hands is my destiny: Help me according to Your mercy, and leave me not to perish in my transgressions, nor allow me to follow them who place desires of the flesh over those of the spirit. I am Your creation; disdain not the work of Your hands. Do not turn away from me; be compassionate and do not humiliate or scorn me, O Lord, as I am weak. I have fled to You as my Protector and God. Heal my soul, for I have sinned against You. Save me for Your mercy's sake, for I have cleaved unto Your from my youth; let me who seeks You not be put to shame by being rejected for my unclean actions, unseemly thoughts, and unprofitable remembrances. Drive away from me every filthy thing and excess of evil. For You alone are holy, mighty, and immortal, and posses sovereign might, which, through You, is given to all those who strive against the devil and the might of his armies. For unto You is due all glory, honor and worship: To the Father, and to the Son, and to the Holy Spirit, now and ever, and unto ages of ages. Amen.

Prayer for Someone in Trouble

O God, our help and assistance, who are just and merciful, and who hears the supplications of Your people, look down upon me, a miserable sinner; have mercy upon me, and deliver me from this trouble that besets me, for which, I know, I am deservedly suffering.

I acknowledge and believe, O Lord, that all trials of this life are given by You for our chastisement when we drift away from You and disobey Your commandments.

Deal not with me after my sins, but according to Your bountiful mercies, for I am the work of Your hands, and You know my weakness.

Grant me, I beseech You, Your divine helping grace, and endow me with patience and strength to endure my tribulations with complete submission to Your will.

You know my misery and suffering, and to You, my only hope and refuge, I flee for relief and comfort, trusting to in your infinite love and compassion that, in due time, according to Your good pleasure, You will deliver me from this trouble and turn my distress into comfort, when I shall rejoice in Your mercy and exalt and praise Your holy name, O Father, Son and Holy Spirit, now and ever and unto ages of ages.

PRAYERS FOR PURITY

Prayer by Mark the Monk

O undefiled, pure, all-merciful Lord, Who in taking on humanity freed our nature from corruption; and by uniting it with that which is superior totally sanctified it; You who grant the riches of your grace to those who confidently believe in You; You who shamed that ancient and arrogant one who tripped us up in the weakness of the flesh; do You, the same benevolent Lord, cleanse me who am passionate and sin-loving, and who has been defiled by imaginings during sleep, and of every impurity of body and soul. Do not account this to me as a sin, whether I was defiled by a dream borne of the malice of that unnamed and god-hating demon, or whether by immoderation in hurtful things, or whether by evil habit and overbearing presumption. From this time forward, strengthen me against his sinister rage by means of Your all-powerful grace and preserve me against his various evil plans, maintaining the lamp of my chastity undimmed unto the end. So that, being rescued from the attack of abominable passions and from the fearsome gloom of nighttime fantasies by Your power, may I meditate day and night upon the luminous vision of Your judgments, which are sweeter and more to be desired than honey and the honey-comb; and with purity of conscience, I may be deemed worthy to participate in Your life-giving and immortal Mysteries. Through the intercession of Her who bore You without corruption, our most-pure Lady, the Theotokos and Ever-virgin Mary, and all of the Saints. Amen.

Prayer by Saint Basil the Great

O all-merciful, incorrupt, pure, undefiled, only sinless Lord, cleanse me, Your useless servant from all defilements of body and soul, and from this impurity which happened to me because of my carelessness and indifference, together with my other iniquities. Purify me of every stain by the grace of Your Christ; sanctify me by sending down Your Holy Spirit; so that, rising up from the fog of my impurities and the fantasies of the devil, and from every diabolical defilement, I might be made worthy in pure conscience to open my foul and polluted mouth to praise Your all-holy Name of the Father, the Son, and the Holy Spirit; and thereby to participate guiltlessly and uncondemned in the most pure, immortal, most holy and life-giving Mysteries of Your only-begotten Son, our Lord, God and Savior Jesus Christ; with Whom You are blessed, together with Your all holy, and good, and life-creating Spirit, now and ever, and unto ages of ages. Amen.

Another Prayer for Purity

Again have I the wretched one been tripped up in my mind by serving my evil and sinful habits. Again I am dragged as a captive by the prince of darkness and the father of passionate pleasure; and as a slave, humiliated by his will, he forces me to serve the desires of the flesh. And what am I to do, O Lord, O Lord, redeemer and defender of all who hope in You; but to turn again to You, and sigh, and beg forgiveness for the things which I have done. But I fear and tremble that perhaps, even though I confess daily and try to avoid harmful things, yet still I persist in sin every hour, and fail to render my prayer to You, my God, and thus Your patient might be turned to wrath. And who can bear Your anger, O Lord? Wherefore, knowing the multitude of Your compassions and the abyss of Your love for mankind, again I throw myself upon Your mercy, and I cry to You, saying: I have sinned, O Lord; have mercy upon me, the fallen one. Grant unto me Your hand in help, who am sunk in the pit of pleasures; and do not abandon me, O Lord, Your servant, to be destroyed by my iniquities and my sins. Rather, in Your usual goodness deliver me from the pollution and the stain of my flesh and from my passionate thoughts which in every way defile my miserable soul. Behold, O Lord my God, there is not even one place in it that is clean, but it is altogether leprous; my body is itself one great wound. Therefore, as the healer of souls and the wellspring of life, cleanse my soul with tears which You shall pour out upon me abundantly. Grant me healing and cleansing, and do not turn Your face from me, lest the darkness of despair consume me as fire. But as You, the all-true God, said: there is joy in heaven at the return of one sinner. Close not the ears of Your compassion against the prayer of my repentance; but open them unto me and direct my prayer before You as incense. You, the Creator, knows the weakness of our nature, how easily we slip in our youth; yet You overlook the sins and You accept the repentance of those who confess to You in truth. For Thou alone are sinless, and unto You we ascribe glory, now and ever, and unto ages of ages. Amen.

PRAYERS FOR SPIRITUAL GUIDANCE

Prayer to Find a Spiritual Father,
by Saint Symeon the Theologian, the New

O Lord, who does not desire the death of a sinner but that he should turn and live, You who came down to earth in order to restore life to those lying dead through sin and in order to make them worthy of seeing You the true light as far as is possible to man, send me a man who knows You, so that in serving him and subjecting myself to him with all my strength, as to You, and in doing Your will in his, I may please You the only true God, and so that even I, a sinner, may be worthy of Your Kingdom. Amen.

Prayer Before Reading Holy Books,
by Saint John Chrysostom

In the name of the Father, and of the Son, and of the Holy Spirit:

Master, Lover of mankind, make the pure light of your divine knowledge shine in our hearts and open the eyes of our mind to understand the message of your Gospel. Implant in us the fear of your blessed commandments, so that, having trampled down all carnal desires, we may change to a spiritual way of life, thinking and doing all things that are pleasing to you. For you are the illumination of our souls and bodies, Christ God, and to you we give glory, together with your Father who is without beginning, and your all-holy, good and life-giving Spirit, now and for ever, and to the ages of ages. Amen.

O Lord Jesus Christ, open the eyes of my heart, that I may hear Your word and understand and do Your will, for I am a sojourner upon the earth. Do not hide Your commandments from me, but open my eyes, that I may perceive the wonders of Your law. Speak to me of the hidden and secret things of Your wisdom. I have set my hope on You, my God, that You enlighten my mind and understanding with the light of Your knowledge, not only to cherish those things which are written, but to do them, that in reading the lives and sayings of the Saints I may not sin, but that they may serve for my restoration, enlightenment and sanctification, for the salvation of my soul, and the inheritance of life everlasting; For You are the enlightenment of those who lie in darkness, and from You comes every good deed and every gift. Amen.

Prayer for Priests

O Lord Jesus Christ, set the hearts of all Your priests on fire with zealous love for Your, that they may ever seek Your glory; Give them strength that they may labor unceasingly in Your earthly vineyard for the salvation of our souls and the glory of Your All-Honorable and Majestic Name of the Father, and of the Son, and of the Holy Spirit, now and ever, and unto ages of ages. Amen.

PRAYERS FOR THE SICK

Prayers for Others Who are Sick

O Lord our God, the Physician of our souls and bodies, look down upon Your servant *(name)* and cure *him/her* of all infirmities of the flesh, in the Name of our Lord and Savior Jesus Christ, with Whom You are blessed, together with Your Most Holy, Gracious, and Life-giving Spirit, always, now and forever, and unto ages of ages. Amen.

O Merciful Lord, visit and heal Your sick servant, *(name)*, now lying on the bed of sickness and sorely afflicted, as You, O Saviour, once raised Peter's mother-in-law and the paralytic who was carried on his bed: for You alone have borne the sickness and afflictions of our race, and for You nothing is impossible, and are all-merciful. Amen.

Prayer for Oneself when Sick

O Lord Jesus Christ our Saviour, Physician of our souls and bodies, Who became Man and suffered death on the Cross for our salvation, and through Your tender love and compassion healed all manner of sickness and affliction: Lord, visit me in my suffering, and grant me grace and strength to bear this sickness with which I am afflicted, with Christian patience and submission to Your will, trusting in Your loving kindness and tender mercy. Bless the means used for my recovery, and those who administer them. I know, O Lord, that I justly deserve any punishment You might inflict upon me, for I have so often offended You and sinned against You in thought, word, and deed. Therefore, I humbly pray that You look upon my weakness, and not deal with me according to my sins, but according to the multitude of Your mercies. Have compassion on me, and let mercy and justice meet; and deliver me from the sickness and suffering I am undergoing. Grant that my sickness may be the means of my true repentance and amendment of my life according to Your will, that I may spend the rest of my days in Your love and fear; that my soul, being helped by Your grace and sanctified by Your holy mysteries, may be prepared for its transition to eternal life and there, in the company of Your blessed saints, I may praise and glorify You with Your Eternal Father and Life-giving Spirit. Amen.

Prayers for Thanksgiving After Recovery

Almighty God, our Heavenly Father, the Source of life and Fountain of all good things, I bless Your Holy Name, and offer to You my most hearty thanks for having delivered me from my sickness and restored me to my health.

Grant me Your grace, and I pray that you enable me to keep my resolutions, and correct the errors of my past life, that I may improve in virtue, and live a new life in dutiful fear of You, doing Your will in all things, devoting this new life that You have given me to Your service, that so by living for You, I may be ready, when it pleases You to call me to You, our Heavenly Father, who, together with Your Only-Begotten Son, our Lord Jesus Christ, and Your Life-giving Spirit, are due all honor, glory, praise, and thanksgiving: now and forever, and unto ages of ages. Amen.

Prayers After an Operation

Holy Father, the only true physician of our souls and bodies, who cast down and lift up, accept me as I come in all humility to glorify you and thank you for preserving, by your grace, your servant *(Name)* through *his/her* recent operation.

We thank you for blessing the attending physicians and the means employed for *his/her* cure, and for restoring *his/her* safe and sound to *his/her* family and Church, having fended off every danger against *his/her* body and soul.

Raise *him/her* speedily, we pray you, from the bed of illness on which *he/she* lies and return *him/her* to *his/her* home and peaceful pursuits. Grant that the suffering of *his/her* body may avail for the purifying of *his/her* soul and may lead *him/her* to return, in thanksgiving, to the works of *his/her* hands and to Christ Jesus, the Physician of soul and body.

Through the prayers of our Holy Fathers, Lord Jesus Christ our God have mercy on us and save us. Amen.

Prayer the Terminally Ill

Lord, Jesus Christ, Who suffered and died for our sins that we may live, if during our life we have sinned in word, deed or thought forgive us in Your goodness and love. All our hope we put in You; protect your servant *(name)* from all evil. We submit to Your will and into Your hands we commend our souls and bodies. For a Christian end to our lives, peaceful, without shame and suffering, and for a good account before the awesome judgment seat of Christ, we pray to you O Lord. Bless us, be merciful to us and grant us life eternal. Amen.

PRAYERS FOR TRAVELERS

Prayer Before Travel

Lord Jesus Christ our God, be my Companion, guide and protector during my journey. Keep me from all danger, misfortune and temptation. By Your divine power grant me a peaceful and successful journey and safe arrival. In You I place my hope and trust and You I praise, honor and glorify, together with Your Father and Holy Spirit now and forever and ever. Amen.

Another Prayer Before Travel

Lord Jesus, You traveled with the two disciples after the resurrection and set their hearts on fire with Your grace. Travel also with me and gladden my heart with Your presence. I know, Lord, I am a pilgrim on this earth, seeking the citizenship which is in heaven. During my journey surround me with Your holy angels and keep me safe from seen and unseen dangers. Grant that I may carry out my plans and fulfill my expectations according to Your will. Help me to see the beauty of creation and to comprehend the wonder of Your truth in all things. For You are the way, the truth and the life, and to You we give thanks, praise and glory forever. Amen.

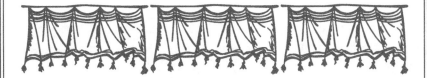

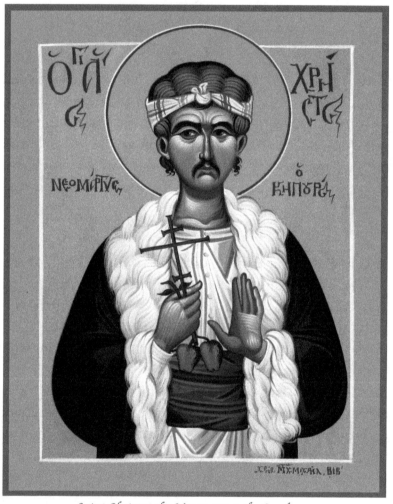

Ὁ ΆΓ⟨ΙΟⳞ⟩ ΧΡΗⳞΤⲤⳞ
ΝΕΟΜΆΡΤΥⳞ ὁ ΚΗΠΟΥΡ⟨Ⳟ⟩

Saint Christos the Newmartyr, the Gardener

THE FASTING PERIODS
OF THE CHURCH

When we should Abstain

Fasting Categories:

Category A. Abstain from meats and poultry products.

Category B. Abstain from dairy products, (milk, yogurt, cheese etc...) *[includes category A]*

Category C. Abstain from fish products. *[includes category A and B]*

Category D. of Wine and oil, includes cuttlefish, calamari, octopus etc... *[includes category A, B & C]*

Category E. Strict Fast. No oil in foods, boiled pulses (lentils, chickpeas, etc...), beans, pasta etc... *[includes category A, B, C, & D]*

Days on which the faithful must fast:

1. Every Wednesday and Friday. *(Cat. E)*.

2. Great Lent [from clean Monday till Holy Easter Saturday.] *(Cat. E. except Saturdays and Sundays which are Cat. D.)*

3. Apostles Fast. [from the Monday after Sunday of All Saints till 28th June.] *(Cat. D. except Saturday And Sunday where Cat. C is allowed.)*

4. The 15 Day fast of the Holy Virgin Mary. [1st August-14th August.] *(Cat. E. Except Sat and Sun. Cat. D.)*

5. The 40 day Nativity fast. *[from 15th Nov. - 24th Dec. The Church allows fasting from Nov. 15th - Dec. 7th to be Cat. C., except of course on Wednesdays and Fridays which is Cat. E; from 18th Dec 18th - Dec 23rd must be Cat. D].*

6. Strict fasts *(Cat. E)* have the following days unless they fall on a Sat. or Sunday., when they become relaxed *(Cat. D)*:

5th January *(Eve of Theophany)*

29th August *(Beheading of St. John the Baptist)*

14th September *(Elevation of the Holy Cross)*

Non Fast Days, when fasting is not allowed, even if they fall on Wednesdays and Fridays:

The Days after the Nativity. *(25th Dec. till 4th Jan)*

The first week of Triodion, that is the week following Sunday of Pharisee and the Publican.

The week after Pascha. *(Renewal Week)*

The week after Pentecost. *(Holy Spirit week)*

Two Category Fasts.

Meatfare and Cheesefare week. No meat 1st and 3rd week of the Triodion.

If a Major Feast Day or a Saint's day fall on Fasting Periods, they change as follows:

25th March, Annunciation; 24th June, Birth of the Forerunner, 6th August, Transfiguration day - *become Cat. C fasts with fish is allowed.*

Fish is allowed on the following days, even if they fall on a Wednesday or Friday *(Cat. C.)*:

7th January, Synaxis of the Forerunner.

2nd February, Presentation of Christ.

29th June, Saints Peter and Paul.

15th August, Dormition of the Most Holy Theotokos.

8th September, Birth of the Most Holy Theotokos.

14th November, Apostle Phillip.

21st November, The Entry of the Theotokos into the Temple.

Wednesday of Mid-Pentecost.

Wednesday before the Ascension of Christ *(last day of the feast of Easter)*

The following dates become Cat. D. *(wine and oil allowed)*, even if they fall on a Wednesday, a Friday or during fasting periods.

In the Month of:

January: 11th, 16th, 17th, 20th, 22nd, 25th, 27th, 30th.

February, 8th, 10th, 11th, 17th, 24th.

March, 9th, 26th.

April, 23rd, 25th, 30th.

May, 2nd, 8th, 15th, 21st, 25th.

June, 8th, 11th, 30th.

July, 1st, 2nd, 17th, 20th, 22nd, 25th–27th.

August: 31st.

September: 1st, 6th, 9th, 13th, 20th, 23rd, 26th.

October: 6th, 18th, 23rd, 26th.

November: 1st, 8th, 12th, 13th, 16th, 25th, 30th.

December: 4th, 5th, 6th, 9th, 12th, 15th, 17th, 20th.

All Wednesdays and Fridays in the period of Pentecost become *Cat. D* fasts.

GLORY BE TO GOD. AMEN.

*Lord Jesus Christ, Son of God,
Have mercy on us.*

Most, Holy Theotokos, Save us.

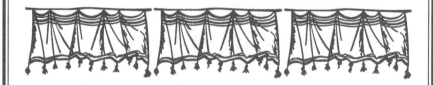

PASCHALION

	TRIODION BEGINS	MEATFARE	ANNUNCIATION	LATIN PASCHA	ORTHODOX PASCHA	ASCENSION	PENTECOST	ALL-SAINTS	APOSTLE'S FAST
2013	Feb-24	Mar-10	M-1	Mar-31	May-5	Jun-13	Jun-23	Jun-30	4 Days
2014	Feb-9	Feb-23	Tu-4	Apr-20	Apr-20	May-29	Jun-8	Jun-15	13 Days
2015	Feb-1	Feb-15	W-5	Apr-5	Apr-12	May-21	May-31	Jun-7	21 Days
2016	Feb-21	Mar-6	F-2	Mar-27	May-1	Jun-9	Jun-19	Jun-26	2 Days
2017	Feb-5	Feb-19	Sa-4	Apr-16	Apr-16	May-25	Jun-4	Jun-11	17 Days
2018	Jan-28	Feb-11	Su-5	Apr-1	Apr-8	May-17	May-27	Jun-3	25 Days
2019	Feb-17	Mar-3	M-3	Apr-21	Apr-28	Jun-6	Jun-16	Jun-23	5 Days
2020	Feb-9	Feb-23	W-4	Apr-12	Apr-19	May-28	Jun-7	Jun-14	14 Days
2021	Feb-21	Mar-7	Thu-2	Apr-4	May-2	Jun-10	Jun-20	Jun-27	1 Day
2022	Feb-13	Feb-27	F-3	Apr-17	Apr-24	Jun-2	Jun-12	Jun-19	9 Days
2023	Feb-5	Feb-19	Sa-4	Apr-9	Apr-16	May-25	Jun-4	Jun-11	17 Days
2024	Feb-25	Mar-10	M-2	Mar-31	May-5	Jun-13	Jun-23	Jun-30	4 Days
2025	Feb-9	Feb-23	Tu-3	Apr-20	Apr-20	May-20	Jun-8	Jun-15	13 Days
2026	Feb-1	Feb-15	W-5	Apr-5	Apr-12	May-21	May-31	Jun-7	21 Days

Note: The *Annunciation* column indicates when the feast day is celebrated by DAY of the WEEK and WEEK number of Great Lent. *Example:* Tu-4 = Tuesday, March 25, 4th week of Great Lent. The *Apostle's Fast* column for how many days we fast that year during that period.

Τέλος
καὶ τῷ Θεῷ Δόξα.

NEWROME
PRESS

CPSIA information can be obtained
at www.ICGtesting.com
Printed in the USA
LVHW082346300123
738276LV00014B/215/J